A New Approach to Deconstruct and Destroy the SAT

Conquer the SAT with Curvebreakers

A New Approach to Deconstruct and Destroy the SAT.

Copyright 2020 Curvebreakers Test Prep

curvebreakerstestprep.com

ISBN: 978-1-7353188-0-6

Table of Content

Introduction

Test-Taking And Study Skills

SAT Reading 23

SAT Writing & Language 61

ABOUT THE TEAM/ACKNOWLEDGEMENTS

I would like to thank every Curvebreakers staff member (past and present) for being a part of this journey. Brittany Verlezza, who has been working as a tutor and developing curriculum with Curvebreakers for several years, served as the primary creator and author. While working with students will always be her favorite part of the gig, she was incredibly excited to help create a book that was truly unique by pulling from years of shared experience between us and the rest of the Curvebreakers team. A special thanks to our incredible staff – Nikki, Michelle, Mary, Emily, Anthony, and more – for their insight and contributions. And an especially huge shout out to Jacob for his input and assistance.

FOREWORD FROM THE OWNER OF CURVEBREAKERS, NICK LAPOMA

For the last 14 years standardized tests have been my life. When your sole goal is to teach tests, you must strive to understand them to their core. To truly understand tests is to truly understand their format, scaling, and scoring systems. As you may know, standardized tests are graded on a "curve." This is a statistical concept relating to a bell curve, which is a visualization that shows that a large majority of students will fall within the "bell" of the curve with very few outliers. Those outliers are the highest scorers.

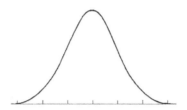

This book shows you how to be an outlier. To do so you do not need to be perfect; you simply need to beat everyone else.

Therein lies the concept of our company "Curvebreakers." We strive to help students break the curve and achieve a higher score. When we started writing this book, our concept was simple: provide you with real, proven strategies that you can implement today. We decided to include no fluff whatsoever. We only included strategies, tips, and tricks that lead to improvement.

That said we are accessible. Feel free to contact us at Info@curvebreakerstestprep.com or call us at (516) 728-1561.

We hope to help you further your educational goals. Now, onto what you came for!

Nick LaPoma

@NickTheTutor on Instagram, Youtube, and Tiktok

Text me at (512) 675- 1516

CHECK US OUT ONLINE

Want more? Curvebreakers offers private tutoring for both standardized tests and subject matter, class instruction, and diagnostic practice tests.

DIAGNOSTIC PRACTICE EXAMS

Taking practice exams is an important part of studying for a standardized exam. Curvebreakers' unique diagnostic score analysis provides insight into test performance by content, question type, and timing. Students with tutoring packages are able to take an *unlimited amount of diagnostic practice exams at no extra charge*.

curvebreakerstestprep.com/practice-exam-dates/

PRIVATE TUTORING

Test Prep: Packages include ACT, SAT, PSAT, SSAT, SHSAT, AP Exams, Regents Exams, ISEE, and CHSEE. If you don't see your exam, please inquire with us. Learn more:

curvebreakerstestprep.com/test-prep

Subject Matter Help: For students who need help throughout the school year or summer to review subject content, Curvebreakers offers separate packages for 3rd - 8th graders and 9th - 12th graders.

curvebreakerstestprep.com/subject-tutoring

CLASSES & EVENTS

Curvebreakers offers classes and one-time events all year round to prepare students for the SAT, ACT, AP Exams, and Regents Exams. Check out our current schedule online:

curvebreakerstestprep.com/eventsexams/

VIDEO COURSES & FREE RESOURCES

Learn the test taking skills and content necessary to succeed with self-paced video courses, and access our collection of free resources.

nickthetutor.thinkific.com

HOW TO USE THIS BOOK

There are two major components to test prep: **practicing problems and understanding the exam.** This book is designed to help with the latter. Much of the discussion will be centered around strategies, tangible things that you can do to sharpen your overall test-taking skills and boost your performance. Many of these skills will apply to all standardized tests, not just the SAT, but **the immediate goal is to build fluency in the language of this particular exam.**

While every SAT is different, the test is **repetitive in nature**. This book will provide an intricate break-down of the exam so that you can recognize these patterns. Before you fight an opponent, you study it; you learn its habits, you recognize its go-to moves. In doing that, you can predict what's coming and deliver an effective counter-move. That's the goal here.

We will discuss the **format** of each section, what **content** you can expect to see, and provide insights to the most **common questions.** That will include different approaches to the questions, information about trick answers (how to spot them and how to avoid them), and some general do's and don'ts to fall back on for each question type.

We will also address foundational skills for each section.. That will include reading and annotating effectively, building essential math skills, utilizing the calculator properly, and using correct grammar and punctuation rules. Use those sections to **assess what skills you may need to work on before or during your preparation for the SAT.**

What you won't find are full practice exams or a large sum of practice questions. There are some sample questions that are designed to familiarize you with the common questions and answer choices. There are also some sample passages to practice essential reading skills. But we find that it's best to leave the business of creating full practice tests and passages to the makers of the SAT!

For that reason, this book is meant to be used in conjunction with real exams and diagnostic reports. Practice, after all, is one of the two core components in test prep, so be sure to work through authentic SAT exams as you read this book. This book can be used at any time — before, during, or after taking the SAT. That being said, your best chance of mastering the exam is by understanding the test **before** you take it.

WHAT IS A GOOD SCORE?

A good score will vary from student to student and depends mostly on the colleges to which you'll be applying . To determine what score you should aim for, first take a diagnostic test and determine your starting score. Next, compare that score to the scores listed by various college admissions offices and decide which ones seem within reach. This target score should be higher than your score on a diagnostic exam, as you can expect your final score to improve after having spent a few months practicing.

You can use the table below as a reference for where you'd rank compared to the rest of test takers at any given score. The table lists the **"percentile rank"** for several scores, which just means the percentage of test takers who scored **less than a given score.** For example, the "percentile rank" of a 1330 is 89, which means 89% of SAT testers scored below a 1330.

For a more detailed list, visit collegeboard.org.

Total Score	SAT User	English Score	SAT User	Math Score	SAT User
1600	99+	800	99+	800	99+
1570	99+	780	99+	780	98
1540	99	760	99	760	97
1510	99	740	98	740	95
1480	98	720	96	720	94
1450	96	700	94	700	92
1420	95	680	91	680	89
1390	93	660	88	660	86
1360	91	640	83	640	83
1330	89	620	78	620	79
1300	86	600	73	600	75
1270	83	580	66	580	69
1240	80	560	60	560	64
1210	76	540	53	540	57
1180	72	520	46	520	49
1150	67	500	39	500	41
1120	62	480	32	480	35
1090	57	460	26	460	29

Total Score	SAT User
1060	51
1030	46
1000	40
970	35
940	30
910	25
880	20
850	16
820	13
790	9
760	6
730	4

English Score	SAT User
440	20
420	14
400	10
380	6
360	3
340	2
320	1

Math Score	SAT User
440	23
420	18
400	13
380	9
360	6
340	3
320	2

FREQUENTLY ASKED QUESTIONS

Q: How can I take a practice test?

A: Email us at info@curebreakerstestprep.com and we can email you the materials to take a practice test. We also offer **diagnostic grading** services so you can see **exactly what you need to do to improve your score.**

Q: How often should I take a practice test, and how much time should I spend preparing for a real test ?

A: We suggest that students take a practice test **at least once every 3 weeks** before taking the real SAT or ACT. We suggest this considering that our students will usually have **4 to 6 months to prepare for the exam**. That would allow the student to take **5+ practice tests before taking the real test.** Real tests can be found on collegeboard.org

Q: What is a "real" SAT exam?

A: A real SAT is an exam made by the same people that make the SAT you are taking, or a test from a prior administration of the exam that they make available online.

Q: How is the exam graded?

A: There are four sections on the exam — Reading, Writing and Language, Non-Calculator Math and Calculator Math. Each section score is calculated by converting a raw score (the number of questions you answered correctly) into a scaled score. **The scale on each exam will differ.** The reading section and the writing and language section are each **out of 400 points.** Those two sections are **added together** to create the Evidence-based Reading and Writing score (out of 800). This is more commonly referred to as the "English" score. The number of raw points from **BOTH** math sections (calculator and non-calculator) combined is used to create a single math score **out of 800 points**. Your composite score is determined by adding the English score and the Math score. **The total score is out of 1600.**

Q: What is superscoring?

A: Superscoring allows you to **compile one "superscore" using your best math score and English score from several test administrations.**

Ex: **Test 1:** 650 English, 680 Math, 1330 Total
         Test 2: 690 English, 660 Math, 1350 Total
         Superscore: 690 English, 680 Math, 1370 Total

For a vast majority of universities, you will only be able to use the **overall** math and English scores; you cannot pick from your highest reading and writing and language scores or combine your best calculator math and non-calculator math performances. Not all colleges accept superscoring. **Check with individual colleges to see their respective policies.** This information can usually be found on their website.

Q: How many times should I take an official SAT?

A: That will depend on a few different factors, but most students will typically sit **for 2–3 official exams.** Some students will require more exams to hit their goals, and that's perfectly acceptable. A common misconception is that colleges frown upon students taking the exam several times. It is only a red flag if the results are wildly inconsistent, which can send a message that the student did not take the exam seriously.

Q: When should I take my first official exam?

A: You'll want to give yourself a few months to prepare before you take your first exam. You should complete **at least 15-20 hours of studying** and take **several practice exams** before your first official test.

One of the more overlooked parts of studying for the SAT is the mental preparation required to succeed. All too often students pile intense pressure on themselves and lose hope if they are not progressing as well as they would have liked. Outside factors such as family, friends, and the looming college acceptance cycle all heavily weigh on the minds of students. This will often lead to lower test results. That said, students can avoid outside stressors and gain mental fortitude with the right approach.

First, you cannot put too much pressure on yourself. As stated before, a "good" score is relative to where you start and where your goals lie. Instead of trying to jump directly to your goal score, you should try to move your score up in 50-point stepping stones. This way, you have less chance of severe disappointment..

Second, you need to take the opinions of family and friends with a grain of salt. **You** are the one who needs to take the test, not them. Of course we love our parents and we understand that they simply want us to succeed, but it is very important to find our own motivation to take these tests. The students that want a better score for themselves typically get greater score increases because their motivation is more genuine. If you are simply studying for the SAT to make your parents happy, it will be difficult to stay motivated.

During the test, it is extremely important to move past mistakes and slip-ups. Great test takers do not dwell on the past but simply move on to the next problem just as they did the last. Most of us will be getting many questions wrong on these tests, so it is important to have the right mental approach. Don't let a bad passage or question get you down. Move past it confidently and remember that every new question is a new opportunity.

If you can reduce outside stressors, become self-motivated, and move past mistakes quickly, you will have a much greater chance of success on test day.

TRACK YOUR PROGRESS

If you haven't already, you should **begin by taking a <u>timed</u>, <u>full-length</u> diagnostic exam.** Those results will help you set some short-term and long-term goals.

Again, you should take full-length practice tests every few weeks (although you may find that more frequent exams will benefit you) and record your results here. Be sure to focus on the individual section scores as well the overall score so that you can assess which sections are improving and which ones still need the most work.

STARTING SCORE

Date Taken	Exam Name	Reading Score	W&L Score	Math Score	Composite Score

*Remember, your composite score is the average of the four section scores. This score is rounded.

PRACTICE TESTS

Date Taken	Exam Name	Reading Score	W & L Score	Math Score	Composite Score

OFFICIAL TESTS

Date Taken	Exam Name	Reading Score	W & L Score	Math Score	Composite Score

Setting reasonable, **incremental** goals is important.

Big changes to your overall score will not happen overnight; it will take time before you see consistent improvements to each of the sections in a way that will boost the composite score. This is not meant to spook you! Before you begin the test prep process, it's important for you to recognize that your improvement may not always be linear. Composite scores may stay the same or even dip down a bit from time to time, but that is normal! The exam is made up of four sections, so increases in one section (although great!) may not impact your total score in the way you might hope.

That said, with the correct approach, a strong game plan, the right mindset, and sheer determination, we have seen students substantially raise their score. Typically the largest score increases come from students who dedicate six months to a year studying and also have the guidance of an expert. If you follow the guidance of this book, you will improve your score. For more advice on how to improve, visit our website.

ASSIGNMENTS

Whether you're working with a tutor or working independently, you should **carve out time each week for SAT prep.** Multiple times a week is even better to keep you continuously immersed in the language of the exam! You can keep track of your assignments here.

DATE   ASSIGNMENT   _____

_____   _____

DATE   ASSIGNMENT   _____

_____   _____

DATE   ASSIGNMENT   _____

_____   _____

DATE   ASSIGNMENT   _____

_____   _____

DATE   ASSIGNMENT   _____

_____   _____

DATE   ASSIGNMENT   _____

_____   _____

DATE   ASSIGNMENT   _____

_____   _____

DATE   ASSIGNMENT   _____

_____   _____

DATE   ASSIGNMENT   _____

_____   _____

DATE   ASSIGNMENT   _____

_____   _____

DATE   ASSIGNMENT   _____

_____   _____

DATE

_____

DATE

_____

DATE

_____

DATE

_____

DATE

_____

DATE

_____

DATE

_____

DATE

_____

DATE

_____

DATE

_____

DATE

_____

DATE

_____

DATE

_____

ASSIGNMENT   _____

_____

ASSIGNMENT   _____

_____

ASSIGNMENT   _____

_____

ASSIGNMENT   _____

_____

ASSIGNMENT   _____

_____

ASSIGNMENT   _____

_____

ASSIGNMENT   _____

_____

ASSIGNMENT   _____

_____

ASSIGNMENT   _____

_____

ASSIGNMENT   _____

_____

ASSIGNMENT   _____

_____

ASSIGNMENT   _____

_____

ASSIGNMENT   _____

_____

DATE   ASSIGNMENT   _____

_____   _____

DATE   ASSIGNMENT   _____

_____   _____

DATE   ASSIGNMENT   _____

_____   _____

DATE   ASSIGNMENT   _____

_____   _____

DATE   ASSIGNMENT   _____

_____   _____

DATE   ASSIGNMENT   _____

_____   _____

DATE   ASSIGNMENT   _____

_____   _____

DATE   ASSIGNMENT   _____

_____   _____

GENERAL TEST-TAKING STRATEGIES

One often overlooked but important aspect of prepping for the SAT is **general standardized test strategy**. Most students want to dive right in to the questions but will overlook basic principles that can substantially impact their score. We will go over those here:

- Time management

    - It is essential that you not only know the exact number of minutes you have per passage or question on the SAT, but that you practice under those time constraints. Proper time management will not always mean working faster, but **working smarter** by **skipping difficult questions and prioritizing certain passages/questions.** Develop a plan for how you will split your time on test day and be sure that you keep an eye on the clock.

- Prioritize

    - All of the questions are worth the same number of raw score points, so it is in your best interest to **complete the easy questions first** or **pick and choose which questions you can complete when time is running out.** "Easy," of course, is a relative term. What you might find simple, someone else may find challenging. **Figure out your own unique strengths and weaknesses** so that you can spend your time wisely on the questions likely to award you points.

- Answer every question

    - There is no penalty for wrong answer choices so you should **put down an answer for every single question** on the exam regardless of time. If you have to guess on a grid-in math question, try "2." Two has several powerful mathematical properties, which makes it a fairly common answer and a great candidate for a random guess.

- Process of elimination

    - Sometimes, a question will have several answer choices that are **absurd** or can be **disproven** by various means (we will discuss this in greater detail later). You should **strike out those answers** on the page and take them out of consideration. This will greatly **improve your chances when randomly guessing**.

- Knowing what's wrong is just as important as knowing what's right

    - As discussed in the last point, eliminating all of the wrong answer choices in a problem is just as valid as selecting the correct answer. The SAT loves to include answer choices that are *mostly* correct in hopes that you will ignore the problematic parts (harshly worded, not relevant to the question, partly incorrect, etc.) Being able to **pinpoint these issues as grounds for elimination** is crucial. You may find that eliminating the three bad answer choices is how you arrive at the correct answer for a fair amount of the questions.

- Remember that there is only one correct answer to every question

  - The SAT is a standardized test, which means there's no room for debate or subjectivity. **There are rules (both written AND unwritten) that you will need to learn and follow.** This should keep you from internally debating certain answer choices based on *preference*. For example, the SAT will always favor concise and non-redundant answers in the English section, so if you start to say to yourself that *YOU* would write with more words or repeat certain words for emphasis, you're likely going in the wrong direction.

- Read every answer choice

  - You should read each of the answer choices, even if you think you've found the correct one. You may find something better! It may seem like a waste of time, but you should **consider all of your options**. The exam will often include answer choices that are *mostly* correct as distractor answers. You may not recognize the flaws in those choices until you are presented with a better one. Take those few extra seconds to ensure that you have picked the **best possible answer**.

- Use your pencil actively

  - You will hear this piece of advice a lot throughout this book. Such a large portion of this exam will test your ability to **filter out important information quickly and precisely.** You don't get to highlight, color code, or use any of the other visual tools that help our eyes distinguish what's important. All you have is your pencil. Use it wisely to boost your attention to detail! Reading comprehension and detail-orientedness is built into every section of the exam (not just the reading section), so it's crucial that you give yourself as many visual cues as possible to ensure you are reading the questions, answers, and passages carefully.

- Abide by a 5-second rule (or something close to it)

  - We will talk a lot about the importance of time management throughout this book. You cannot allow yourself to linger on questions that are not going your way. You will need to **skip them and return only if time remains.** That can be a difficult habit to stick to, so you can follow a "5-second rule." That doesn't mean you should be able to finish a problem in 5 seconds! If after 5 seconds, or at any time during the solving of a question, you have no idea what to do – you can't think of a formula/ procedure, you can't identify what the underlying topic is, you can't spot any clues in the wording of the question or answer choices, you can't figure out where to locate the information, etc. – you should skip it and look to return in the event that time allows.

STUDY TIPS

- Mark up your assignments (**not just wrong answers, but guesses**)

  - Many students make the mistake of "guessing" on a problem, getting it correct, and simply moving on. Those questions must be **analyzed** and **discussed** so you can understand *why* that particular solution or answer is correct. This will ensure that you can answer similar questions correctly on a consistent basis.

- Categorize/label questions by topic

  - Categorization is one of the most important skills for a standardized test. For example, when faced with a grammar question where all of the answer choices are uses (or misuses) of colons and semicolons, you could categorize that question as a punctuation question within the subsection of colons and semicolons. This type of labeling will help you become **fluent in the language of the exam**. Once you know the topic with which you are dealing, you will know exactly how to tackle the problem and **what trap answers to identify and avoid.**

- Time yourself

  - As previously stated, you should **time yourself** not only on full exams, but on partial assignments such as reading passages or science passages. This will help you get used to completing the work within the exam's time constraints.

- Set aside time every week to work on SAT prep

  - **Consistently chipping away at SAT material is the best way to prepare.** As we stated earlier, students that prepare for 6 months or more by studying, taking practice tests, and reading supplementary materials will perform better than students who cram their prep into one or two months. If you **set aside "SAT study time" in your schedule**, you will be more focused on the SAT and have the organizational skills to get the work done.

SAT READING

WHAT'S THE GIST?

The reading section is the first portion of the exam. It's also the longest in both duration and question count. You will have **65 minutes** to complete **52 questions**. The section is broken down into five passages, each containing 10-11 questions.

Each question is a multiple choice question with 4 possible answer choices.

WHAT CAN YOU EXPECT TO SEE?

There are three types of passages you can expect to see: U.S. and world literature, history/social studies, and science. While the first passage is always the literary passage, the order in which the remaining passages are presented to you will vary from test to test.

You will also be given one "paired passage" containing two smaller excerpts. Any one of the five passages can be presented to you in this manner.

- **U.S. and World Literature:** 1 passage (10 questions)

  - Common questions include: main idea/theme, narrator's tone/intent, characterization of relationships/characters, which questions are or are not answered in passage, plot questions

- **History/Social Studies:** 2 passages, or 1 passage and 1 pair (10-11 questions)

  - Common questions include: main idea/theme, narrator's point of view/tone, contrasts between different views/methods mentioned, which statements the author(s) is likely to agree with

- **Science:** 2 passages, or 1 passage and 1 pair (10-11 questions)

  - Common questions include: paraphrasing information found in the passage, locating specific details and drawing reasonable conclusions, relating graphs/charts to underlying arguments

Common questions will include:

- **Big Picture:** Identify the the author's point of view, the primary purpose of the passage, and the rhetorical strategies used by the author
- **Evidence Support:** Cite the part of the passage that supports the answer to the previous question
- **Vocabulary In-Context Questions:** Determine meanings of words in context
- **Data Reasoning:** Accurately read graphs/charts and relate them to the passage
- **Function:** Understand structure of the passage and reason behind the author's phrasing
- **Author's Voice:** Establish author's mood, tone, and point of view
- **Passage Structure:** Determine layout of passage (recognize shifts in discussion)
- **Details:** Find and interpret details
- **Inference:** Draw reasonable conclusions from given information
- **Comparative Relationships:** Interpret similarities and differences between arguments

STRATEGIES

The reading section can be overwhelming if you try to absorb every last detail of the passages; this can mentally exhaust you and/or cause you to run out of time. A deep level of understanding is not necessary to perform well on the questions, so you may need to rethink how you're physically reading through these texts. This section is testing your ability to **quickly** and **efficiently** filter out the important information. That's a skill best learned through continued practice, so be prepared to work through several reading passages.

Let's discuss some general strategies before we get into the specifics. First things first, **you want to prioritize the "easier" passages.** "Easy" is going to mean different things to different people. Some of you might find that more scientific, data-driven passages are simpler. Some of you might find that the literary narratives, which are more about picking up on tone and mood, are easier. You'll want to work through a few exams and figure out which passages are best for YOU.

Perhaps even more importantly, you'll want to determine which one is the worst. That's probably the one you should save for last. Time can be an important factor on this section: even if everything is running smoothly, you may find that you're pressed for time on the last passage of the set. Even if you're not low on time, you'll probably be low on energy. You want to make sure this happens on your weakest passage, not your strongest. For most students, the **historical passages** are typically the most challenging, so you may want to consider leaving this one for last.

You might not find that one passage *type* is any easier than the other. It might come down to the specific topics that are presented to you on any given test. Which brings us to our next strategy: **read the introductory blurbs at the top of each passage.** They will give you an idea of what the passage is about, which might help you decide whether or not you'd like to read through that passage right away or return to it at a later time. The blurbs can also provide you with some great contextual information, like who wrote the passage and when. Perspective can be crucial to your understanding of a passage, *especially* those that are historical in nature.

Passages that contain shorter paragraphs are usually easier and faster to read through. That's something to consider on a test-by-test basis.

Note: There is no one-size-fits-all strategy for the reading section. There are several effective ways to order and read through the passages. What works for the majority may not work for you. You might decide to save your strongest/easiest passage for last because it's the one you can tackle confidently in a short time frame. The important thing is always to figure out what works best for you.

··

Let's discuss how to physically read through the passages. In general, you want to **read for the gist.** There are certain parts of a passage that are not important to focus on during the first read-through, like the specific details. You want to walk away from a passage knowing what the main talking points are, what the overall structure and layout of the passage are, and, if applicable, what the author's tone and perspective are.

You can usually get a pretty good sense of these things if you **focus on the introduction, the conclusion, and the first and last sentence of each paragraph (I.F.L.C.).** Think about it logically for a moment: the opening and closing statements in a passage or paragraph usually highlight what the main idea is. That's what we care about! The middle portion of a paragraph will mostly contain details, the proof that helps to back up the author's point. But we will only read that *carefully* if and when the questions ask for specific details. During the first read, we want to know what the <u>overall</u> arguments are and where in the passage those discussions are brought up.

That does not mean we should ignore the information in the other sentences. You'll develop a sense for what information you should pay attention to, and what information is fluff. Common transition words — those like "however," "therefore," "nevertheless"— usually indicate that a <u>significant</u> point is about to be made and that you should pay closer attention to what follows.

After you read one or two paragraphs, **stop to think about what the overall idea was.** If you find it helpful, write down a few words next to those paragraphs that indicate what those paragraphs were about. This can be especially helpful for those moments when you skim through details. Since you are not reading those lines closely, one or two words that indicate what the details are *about* can help you locate information more quickly when you get to the questions.

Keep these mental (or physical) notes simple, but not *too* broad. It's not enough to say to yourself "that paragraph was about crops." Dig a little deeper: What about crops? Is the paragraph about new farming techniques? Is it about the benefits of pesticides? Is it about how certain crops grow better in certain climates? That's the level of takeaway you want to have. Do you need to absorb the fact that squash is best grown in a dense soil in eastward-facing rows? No. Skim over those details quickly.

....

Annotate wisely. The idea of annotating can seem overwhelming at first, but with practice it should become a natural part of taking the exam. For the purpose of the SAT, detailed annotations are not necessary and would chew up too much time. You simply want to use annotations to help you <u>visually pinpoint what's important and create a map of where the details are located</u>.

A lot of the anxiety surrounding annotations stems from struggling to determine what's important. . This fear leads students to frantically underline *everything* — but not everything is important! Even a really important sentence is going to contain a lot of language that's not essential to your understanding. The average sentence is 15-20 words long. That probably sounds absurd, and you're not wrong for thinking that. At the end of the day, there's probably only 4 or 5 words that are really important in the sentence. Focus on that language.

One effective tactic for marking up the passages is what we like to call the circle technique. The goal is to circle the important words in each sentence: the whos, whats, wheres, whens, whys, and hows. The benefit to this type of strategy is threefold.It will help you **read more quickly**, as your eye will be more inclined to skim over filler words and look for the important terms The act of circling will also help you to **absorb the main ideas and identify patterns.** Finally, it will provide you **visual clues** for what individual paragraphs — and by extension, the entire passage — is about. If you're asked about the main purpose of a paragraph, you won't need to reread that paragraph. All of the important language will be circled for you.

This tactic can be especially helpful for the historical passages. The language can be very dense and ornate, and the sentences very long and hard to follow. For that reason, we will want to focus on (and mark up) any words or phrases that we *can* make sense of. Those words can help us identify the topic of discussion and how the author feels. Don't worry if you cannot *fully* comprehend their argument; just focus on those key terms. We will discuss this passage in greater detail later.

Regardless of the annotation strategy you use, the important thing is to not over-do it. Again, the goal is for you to walk away from the passage with the main talking points and give yourself a map of where the information is located. Think of your circles, notes, and underlines as the basis for a dictionary. When you get to a question that asks you about a specific detail, you're going to need to "look up" that information in the passage. You should be marking the passages in a way that makes this process easier for YOU, however that may look.

Some helpful things to mark up based on the passage type:

- For science-based passages, <u>numbers, names of scientists, names of studies, and important terms that are defined for you</u> may be important things to circle. If you read through a passage that gives you several numerical values, it's likely that you're going to be asked about at least one. Circling them will draw your eye right back to those values

- For the fiction passage, make note of any <u>shifts in perspective or shifts in timeline</u>. If they provide you with some sort of flash-back or memory, it's very likely they will ask you a question about what event occurs first chronologically.

- For fiction passages or any passages where the author's tone is important, circle <u>any words that convey emotion</u>. Make note of language that gives you a clue about how the characters feel, even if it's not straightforward. The passage might not say directly that someone was disinterested. But it may say that they slumped in their chair and stared blankly at the clock. Those elements of body language or dialogue with other characters can really help you <u>characterize the people and relationships</u> in the story.

- For historical passages, focus on any language that can help you identify the author's stance and their tone. Are they passionate? Angry? Hopeful?

- For all passages, mark up any effective literary devices or quotes. Major shifts in discussion are also important things to make note of.

How to mark up those important items will come down to what you decide is most effective for you. Select a strategy that is not too overwhelming or time consuming. You could:

- Circle or double underline *really* crucial conclusions (or anything that you want the eye to catch like dates, numbers, or names), and underline the more general (but still important) talking points

- Star those shifts in timeline, perspective, or discussion that we were discussing earlier. Or place stars next to full sentences or paragraphs that you think are super important
- Take **brief** notes next to each paragraph to keep yourself focused and to indicate where the details are located

It's important that you work at a reasonable speed. If you don't absorb every bit of the passage, don't default to rereading (or panicking)! You want to keep moving. Trust that you can still perform well with the questions even if you only have a loose understanding of the actual text. Also know that **the questions can actually help to build your understanding of the passage if you tackle them wisely,** which is exactly what we'll be discussing next.

Before we do, let's take a look at an example of a marked up excerpt. You'll notice the notes are incredibly brief and that the markings are there strictly to emphasize the key words and patterns — **and not to interpret the text.**

We live in an age of visual information. Infographics flood the web, driven by accessible platforms that instantly translate information into a variety of graphic forms. News outlets routinely harvest large data sets like the census and election returns into maps and graphs that profile everything from consumer preferences to the political landscape. The current proliferation of visual information mirrors a similar moment in the early nineteenth century, when the advent of new printing techniques coincided with the rapid expansion of education. Schoolrooms from the Atlantic seaboard to the Mississippi frontier made room for the children of farmers as well as merchants, girls as well as boys. Together, these shifts created a robust and highly competitive market for school materials, including illustrated textbooks, school atlases, and even the new genre of wall maps.

examples

shift

No individual exploited this publishing opportunity more than Emma Willard, one of the century's most influential educators. From the 1820s through the Civil War, Willard's history and geography textbooks exposed an entire generation of students to her deeply patriotic narratives, all of which were studded with innovative and creative pictures of information that sought to translate big data into manageable visual forms.

Willard aggressively marketed her "Perspective Sketch" to American educators, believing it to be a crucial break with other materials on the market. As she confidently expressed to a friend in 1844, "In history I have invented the map". She also advocated for her "map of time" as a teaching device because she strongly believed the visual preceded the verbal — that information presented to students in graphic terms would facilitate memorization, attaching images to the mind through the eyes.

Quote

Now, onto the questions! A good understanding of a passage does not guarantee a strong performance on the questions. You will need to be detail-oriented, manage your time well, and prioritize the

<u>questions wisely</u> no matter how well you understood the text. Again, even if you don't fully understand the passage, you can still do well with the questions if you stay calm and approach the questions strategically.

Firstly, you don't necessarily want to complete the questions in order. If your understanding of a passage is a little weak, you shouldn't answer a main purpose question right away (which is usually one of the earlier questions). You'll want to avoid the larger, big-picture questions that require a deeper understanding of the overall passage. Look for vocab-in-context questions, line reference questions, and specific detail questions that you can easily locate in the passage. <u>Every time you revisit the passage to answer these questions, your overall understanding of the passage will grow</u> and then you'll be better prepared to answer those overarching questions.

If a question asks you to recall a detail that you can't immediately locate, don't skim the passage for it right away. Keep it on the back-burner. It's likely you'll come across it when you're looking for the answer to a separate question. After you have answered the questions you feel confident answering, you may be left with one or two of those detail questions. This is a good time to check the clock. If you've already spent your allotted time on the passage, you will want to move on.

If you have some time remaining to search for those details, **skim effectively by reading the first and last sentences of each paragraph.** By skimming this way, your eye is very likely to catch a word or phrase that will help you locate the answer. Those opening/closing lines will also give you a sense of what that particular paragraph is about and whether or not you can expect to find your answer there. If a question asks you about the *benefits* of a particular drug and the first sentence of a paragraph focuses on the *negative* side effects, the answer to the question probably won't be located in that paragraph and you can move along. Keep in mind that the order of the questions is purposeful on the SAT. **They will mostly follow the structure of the passage**, so you can usually figure out where in the passage the necessary information will be based on where the question falls.

Skip around. There's no time to re-skim the passage for every question. So you'll have to figure out which ones to table and come back to. This is especially important if you are running low on time. We will talk about time management a bit more later.

Pay close attention to what the question is asking! This can't be emphasized enough. Circle key words in the question that will help you pinpoint *exactly* what it's asking for. Make sure that whatever answer you select isn't just a true statement, but a true statement that's also <u>relevant to the specific question.</u>

Rely on the process of elimination. You will not always get the satisfaction of reading a question and immediately locating the obviously correct answer choice. Most of the time you'll end up with your answer as a result of paring your options down. Cross out the answer choices that are:

- True statements that do not answer the question
- Too harshly, boldly, or definitively worded (more on that later)
- Partly or wholly incorrect (not supported by the passage)

Knowing what's wrong about an answer choice is just as important as identifying what's right! Do not focus solely on what makes an answer choice good. The test will purposely bait you with answer choices that are *mostly* good in hopes that you will ignore a problem. Don't fall into that trap! You should always be looking to sniff out what those problems are and use that as a means of eliminating the answer choice right away.

Sometimes the meaning behind the answer choice is correct, but the *way* it's worded is problematic. **Don't ignore those issues.** Very **harshly worded answer choices are typically not correct.** This is especially true for characterization questions. If you are asked to characterize a person in a story, you may be able to determine whether the answer should have a positive or negative connotation. But to what extreme? If a character is said to be standoffish and cold, we wouldn't want to select an answer choice that contains a word like "cruel." That language is far too bold for this scenario.

Definitively worded answer choices — ones that contain words like "never" or "always" — should typically be avoided. This is especially true for any science-based discussions. Scientists will very rarely speak in definitive terms.

As a reminder, you should **make sure to read each of the provided answer choices**, *even* if you feel you've found a plausible answer. You may not realize that your first choice was incorrect until you are presented with a better or (at first) equally plausible option. As frustrating as it may be to have two seemingly correct answers, that situation forces us to revisit the options with a **heightened attention to detail**. Once we begin to pick apart the language more thoroughly, we'll find that one of the answers is problematic.

....

Avoid drawing your own conclusions. It's important that you base your decisions off of **evidence from the text** and the *reasonable* inferences that can be made. Many questions may even begin with the phrase "what can reasonably be inferred." That may mean that the answer is not *directly* stated in the text, but that there is still **sufficient evidence** to back your answer. You should **not have to connect too many dots or make conclusions entirely on your own**.

For example, if the text claims that infants typically learn to walk when they are between 11 and 15 months old, we can infer that infants usually cannot walk before they are 11 months old. Even though that wasn't stated for us directly, we can logically make that conclusion based on the evidence provided. What you don't want to do is start a string of thoughts that are not rooted in the facts present. Avoid the "wellll, this *probably* leads to this….and then that *could* mean this…which could *also* mean…" train of thought.

Lastly, **fall back on your general do's and don'ts for the different question types.** We will discuss these in greater detail momentarily. Having these strategic, almost rule-based approaches to the questions will make them feel less subjective. These questions are not meant to be subjective: the information in the passage combined with the overall rules for the exam is all you need to confidently arrive at the correct answer.

MAIN PURPOSE/CENTRAL IDEA QUESTIONS

You will see a handful of these on every exam. They tend to cause students a great deal of stress, but they shouldn't! You don't have to understand a passage in order to answer these questions correctly. Your job is not to interpret the text. Your job is simply to identify what the passage is about and how the information was relayed.

If you have marked up the passage, look at the circled or underlined information and read any notes that you've written down. Think about what the major talking points were. You may remember from our discussion of question prioritization that main purpose questions may not be the best ones to answer right away. In answering the other questions, you will get a real sense for what the main idea of the passage was.

Sometimes you will be asked about the main purpose of the entire passage, and sometimes you will be asked about the main purpose of a single paragraph. The strategy is the same for either type of question: identify the **overall** idea. That means **avoiding specifics**. An extremely detailed answer is not going to touch on the main idea; even if the answer choice is true, it doesn't answer the question of what the MAIN idea is. So it must be eliminated. This circles back to the idea of eliminating true statements that do not directly answer the question.

If an answer choice focuses on information that was only presented halfway through or towards the end of a passage, that is also pretty safe grounds for elimination. Something that was only discussed for a small portion of a passage is not going to touch on the overall idea.

It's not enough to identify the topic of the passage. You must think about how the information is presented to you. **Pay close attention to words like "summary," "analysis," "critique," and "description" in the answer choices.** These words tend to get glossed over, but they are important! There is a big difference between a summary and an analysis. A summary restates information in a concise manner, while an analysis breaks a topic down on a deeper level.

Do's

- Save this question for last if your understanding of the passage is weak
- Use your annotations to identify the overall talking points
- Pay close attention to the wording of the answer choices

Don'ts

- Pick specific, detail-oriented answers
- Select answers that reference information introduced towards the middle/end of the passage

VOCAB-IN-CONTEXT QUESTIONS

These questions will refer you back to a particular line in the passage and ask you how a word or phrase is being used.

These are called vocab-*in-context* for a reason! These questions are <u>not designed to test your preexisting knowledge of the word.</u> In fact, basing these questions off your knowledge of the word will sometimes get you into trouble. You must **base your decision solely on how the word or phrase is being used in this <u>unique</u> situation.** The word might be used in a way that you wouldn't typically think of, and that's okay! Let the situation guide your decision, even if it means using the original word in an unfamiliar way.

The most obvious synonym is usually not correct. Sometimes an obvious synonym may work; if the situation calls for it, don't be afraid to select it. As long as it was the <u>situation</u> that led you to that synonym and not your knowledge of the original word's definition.

Read the sentences before and after the line reference to give yourself those important contextual clues. The sentence containing the word alone won't always give you a strong sense for what point is being made. Reading <u>around</u> the site of the word will help build a stronger understanding of the underlying argument. Once you have that understanding, **pick your own synonym** before looking at the answer choices. The word or phrase you pick doesn't have to be formal language or grammatically correct for the sentence; just find a way to illustrate the idea in your own words. *Then* look at the provided synonyms and pick the one that most closely lines up with your own phrasing.

Be picky with the slight differences in answer choices: those minor differences can have <u>major</u> implications. Words can have very similar meanings but be used in very different ways. Synonyms can be interchangeable in *some* circumstances, but not in others. For example, you can call a Ferrari valuable or expensive: "valuable" and "expensive" both indicate monetary worth in this scenario. You can also refer to time spent with family as "valuable." You can't, however, refer to time spent with family as "expensive." "Valuable" can be applied to a variety of situations, but "expensive" is used exclusively in relation to cost.

Do not default to selecting a synonym just because you're familiar with it. If you know it doesn't really work for this situation, you should use that as a reason to <u>eliminate it</u>. Remember how important the process of elimination is on this exam; these questions are no exception. You're safer choosing a word that's unfamiliar than one that *is* familiar but that simply does not work for the given line reference.

If you're really stuck, try **substituting in the answer choices**. One of them should maintain the original meaning of the sentence better than the others.

In summary, vocab-in-context will always come down to the specific situation at hand. That is ultimately what should direct your decision-making.

Do's

- Read before and after the specific line reference
- Pick your own synonym based on the specific situation
- Pay close attention to the minor differences in the answer choices
- Substitute in the answer choices

Don'ts

- Base your decision solely off the word's common definition
- Select a synonym just because it's familiar to you
- Be afraid of synonyms that use the original word in an "unusual" or unfamiliar way

....

DETAIL EXTRACTION QUESTIONS

A handful of questions will ask you to extract or paraphrase information from the text. If you have actively marked up your document, locating the answer to these questions shouldn't be too difficult. If you have not marked up the text or your markings do not help you locate where this information is, remember that you don't have to answer this question right away; you can keep it on the backburner.

By nature, some of these questions are easier to find than others: the topic of the question may send you back to a very *particular* place in the passage. Others may seem like they could have been introduced at any point in the passage and will be harder to locate as a result. No matter what, you should be revisiting the passage to answer these questions. **Do not rely on your memory.**

Be very detail-oriented when revisiting the passage. Now is not the time to skim! You want to read the passage and answer choices very precisely to make sure they are lining up. You cannot simply match words in the passage to words in the answer choices and assume that they are saying the same thing. You may miss crucial language and contextual clues if you work through these questions too quickly.

Do not default to selecting an answer choice because it contains language that was found close to the site of the question. Information that's nearby might have nothing to do with the actual question! The exam will try to use "bait language" in hopes that you will select an answer choice without actually reading how that language is being used. Avoid these traps by reading carefully.

Do's

- Answer right away if you feel you can easily locate your proof
- Find evidence from the passage

- Reread the passage and the answer choices carefully

Don'ts

- Answer right away if you have no idea where to look for your proof
- Rely solely on your memory of the passage
- Select answers solely because they contain language similar (or identical) to the passage without considering context

....

PAIRED EVIDENCE QUESTIONS

Several detail questions will be paired with an evidence question. The evidence question will ask you to identify the specific line in the text that provides proof of the answer to the previous question. **These questions are best answered simultaneously.** When you are presented with a detail question, take a look at the following question (even if it's on the next page) to determine if it is part of a pair. That will change your approach to the problem.

Note: Not all line reference questions are paired-evidence questions; some are stand-alone questions. Be sure that you take the time to read what each individual question is asking, and **do not assume that ANY question containing line references is paired with the previous question.**

When you are presented with a pair, this is the best approach:

1. Read the first question and its answer choices. Eliminate any that you are certain are wrong (irrelevant to the question; partly or wholly inaccurate, etc.), but do not select an answer

2. Read the line references.

3. Eliminate any references that are not related to the previous questions or any that are "meatless." Some line references may deal with the topic of the previous question, but not say anything of **substance**. We want something with a little meat.

4. Pair the best line reference with an answer choice from the previous question and select both answers.

Note: Some line references may seem effective, but will not have a partner to pair it with for the first question. Those will need to be eliminated as well.

The line reference is usually the easier question to deal with; it often comes down to selecting the line that focuses on the proper topic and says something of substance. That's partly why we encourage you to **answer the line reference question first**. It's also to keep us from trying to answer what could be a difficult detail question on our own. Why comb through the entire passage ourselves or rely on our often unreliable memory when we can revisit 4 precise lines in the passage?

This type of cyclical approach will take some getting used to, but it is an incredibly effective strategy for some of the most common questions found on this section.

Do's

- Check to see if a detail question belongs to a pair
- Work through paired questions simultaneously
- Start by selecting a significant and relevant line reference
- Use that line reference to better understand and answer the previous question.

Don'ts

- Answer the first question before reading the line references
- Assume every question with line references belongs to a pair
- Pick a line reference that mentions the topic at at hand, but does not say anything significant

....

GRAPH READING QUESTIONS

The SAT does not have a designated science section like the ACT does. To compensate for that, graph reading questions will be sprinkled throughout the reading and writing and language sections.

These questions will require you to read the figures carefully to extract accurate information, but they will **often require you to form a connection between the data and the arguments made in the passage as well**. Many of the graph reading questions function as main idea questions and force you to think about how the figures work with the bigger picture. For that reason, it's not always enough to extract an accurate piece of information from the graph; you may need to figure out *how* that information illustrates the points made in the passage and what exactly those points are.

That is, after all, what graphs do: they provide numerical or visual evidence of the argument. You must keep one eye on that argument. You must also **consider the question prompt carefully**. It may specify what elements of the graph you should be looking at. You may have to complete a statement that's already begun or pick an example similar to one that's already been provided, so a careful analysis of the text may also be necessary.

As far as extracting accurate information from the graphs goes, this is more about being **detail-oriented.** You probably feel pretty comfortable reading tables and charts, but that does not mean that these questions are guaranteed points. **Take the time to read the title of the graphs, the axes,**

and any other notes that accompany the figures. Think about what precise information is presented. It's not enough to pull a number from the table. What does that number mean? A percent or average means nothing without context, and that **context is crucial** for answering these questions. Trick answers will take advantage of the students who don't take the time to digest what information is *actually* presented in the figures.

Do's

- Examine the graphs closely: read the title, axes, keys and another other information that will help you identify <u>specifically</u> what is being illustrated
- Think about the big picture. What point is being made in the passage and how does the graph emphasize that point?

Don'ts

- Pick an answer just because it's graphically supported. It may not actually answer the question.
- Work through these questions too quickly. Take your time to read the graphs and answer choices <u>carefully</u>.

MANAGE YOUR TIME

With 65 minutes to complete 5 passages, you'll have **about 13 minutes per passage.** Take that statement with a grain of salt. Some passages may take a little more time, and others a little less.

About 3-4 minutes of that time should be spent reading through the actual text, with the remaining time spent on the questions. As we mentioned earlier, there is no one-size-fits all reading strategy. You may find reading quickly so that you can devote more time to the questions is beneficial for you. Or you may find that a slightly slower read will help you grasp a bit more information and help you work through the questions more confidently. Figure out what works best for you.

Here is a general time management tactic:

Minutes 0 - 3/4: read and mark up the text

Minutes 3/4 - 9/10: work through the questions whose answers are easy to locate (vocab- in-context, line reference questions, certain detail-extraction questions, graph/figure questions)

Minutes 9/10 - 11/12: circle back to bigger-picture questions like main purpose questions

Minutes 11/12- 13: skim the first and last lines of each paragraph in search of any remaining detail- extraction questions

....

The one exception to this format is the paired passage. The paired passage presents two smaller excerpts. For this passage, you should read the first excerpt and then immediately go to the questions that deal exclusively with that excerpt. The SAT will not separate these questions for you; you will have to use your instincts to determine which questions are strictly about the first excerpt. Once you have completed those questions, read the second excerpt and answer the remaining questions; some will be exclusively about the second excerpt and some will require you to compare and contrast the two texts. Even if you do not feel super confident in your ability to compare/contrast, there are plenty of excerpt-specific questions that you can tackle on these passage types!

....

If you find that you are short on time for the final passage, you'll need to skim the text even quicker than normal — you don't want to spend half of your remaining time reading! Utilize the I.F.L.C strategy: read the intro, first and last sentence of each paragraph, and the conclusion. Find short questions that you think you can answer quickly: line reference, vocab questions, really anything that you can do without having much knowledge of the passage.

Ideally, you'll be able to give yourself enough time to work through all 5 comfortably, but that won't always be the case. With continued practice, you should be able to pick up your speed. That won't always mean reading or working faster, but working *smarter*. Learning how to prioritize the questions and skipping over difficult or time consuming questions are important time-saving skills.

No matter what, you should be keeping an eye on the clock. You will need to determine what point to cut off a passage and move onto the next. **Don't make the mistake of waiting too long before you check the time.** It can be really easy to accidentally spend 15 minutes on a passage or two. The literary and historical passages, for example, can be very easy to mismanage your time on. Those mistakes may limit your time on the last passage, possibly even the last 2, which is a hard hole to dig yourself out of.

"The more you read, the more things you will know," writes Dr. Seuss. Books can inspire many forms of intellectual growth in their readers: some might read for knowledge, others for escapism, and still more to uncover deep truths. This kind of reading, however, differs greatly from reading on the SAT. Unlike reading for leisure or reading for assignments, when you're reading on the SAT, you'll want to zero-in on the information that will be tested. You should always pay attention to the passage's **topic, main point, and tone**; certain passage types will demand additional focuses. In this section, you'll learn how to read the different passage types that you will encounter on the SAT.

Recall that the SAT Reading Section always begins with a literary passage. Of the four remaining passages, you'll encounter passages of three categories: U.S. or world literature, natural sciences, and history/social studies. The passage types may appear in any order. One passage will be a "paired passage." The paired passage contains two smaller excerpts that, in some way, communicate. We'll pay special attention to the literary passage, the historical passage, and the paired passage.

....

PROSE FICTION/LITERARY NARRATIVE

A prose passage is an excerpt pulled from a novel or short story. For the prose passage, you will likely be asked questions pertaining to the plot of the passage, so be sure to pay close attention to the plot-driven elements. **Who are the characters? What are they doing? Why are they doing it?** Since these passages are fiction, they will not possess the kinds of factual information that you would find in a passage about whales, economics, or psychology.

Besides the basic plot, you should focus on the **feelings, emotion, and personality traits** present in the passage. Is one character mad at another? Does someone have a peculiar trait or way of doing things? Is someone hopeful that something might happen? Scared of a certain outcome? Excited about a new adventure or change? **This emphasis is unique to the literary passage, so expect questions on these emotional undercurrents.**

Here is an example of a prose passage you might find on the SAT. Read this passage actively as if you were taking the real test. Give yourself a few minutes to read the passage and try to pull out the feelings/emotions involved. In the space provided, jot down some notes as an exercise.

EXERCISE: PASSAGE UNDERSTANDING- PROSE FICTION

Amory Blaine inherited from his mother every trait, except one or two few, that made him worthwhile. His father, Stephen, was a useless, inarticulate man with an odd taste for the poetry of Lord Byron and a habit of drowsing over the Encyclopedia Britannica. Stephen became wealthy at thirty, when his two elder brothers, successful Chicago brokers, died. In the first flush of feeling that the world was his, Amory's father went to

Bar Harbor and met Beatrice O'Hara, and they later wed. Stephen Blaine handed down to posterity his height of just under six feet and his tendency to hesitate at crucial life moments; both of these two traits appeared in Amory. For many years, Stephen hovered in the background of his family's life, an unassertive figure with a face half-obscured by lifeless, silky hair, continually occupied in "taking care" of his wife, and continually harassed by the idea that he didn't, and couldn't, understand her.

But Beatrice Blaine! There was a woman! Early pictures taken on her father's estate at Lake Geneva, Wisconsin, or in Rome a t the Sacred Heart Convent--an educational extravagance that in her youth was only for the daughters of the exceptionally wealthy--showed the exquisite delicacy of her features, the classic artfulness and simplicity of her clothes. A brilliant education she had: her youth passed in renaissance glory, she was versed in the latest gossip of the old families of Rome; and known by name as a fabulously wealthy American girl to Cardinal Vitori and Queen Margherita and other more subtle celebrities. She learned in England to prefer whiskey and soda over w ine, and her small talk was broadened during a winter in Vienna. All in all, Beatrice O'Hara absorbed the sort of education that will be quite impossible to attain ever again: a tutelage measured by the number of things and people one could simultaneously look down on and be charming about; a culture rich in all arts and traditions, but barren of all ideas.

In her more down to earth moments, Beatrice returned to America, met Stephen Blaine and married him--this almost entirely because she was a little bit weary, a little bit sad. Her only child was carried through a tiresome season and brought into the world on a spring day in 1896.

When Amory was five he was already a delightful companion for her. He was an auburn-haired boy, with great, handsome eyes which he would grow into eventually, an easy, imaginative mind and a taste for costumes. From his fourth to his tenth years, he saw the country with his mother in her father's private car; they went from Coronado, where his mother became so bored that she had a nervous breakdown in a fashionable hotel, down to Mexico City, where she developed an almost epidemic case of tuberculosis.

So, while more or less fortunate little rich boys were defying governesses on the beach at Newport, or being spanked or tutored or read to from young boys' classic story books, Amory was biting obliging bell-boys in the Waldorf-Astoria Hotel, outgrowing a natural disgust of chamber music and symphonies, and acquiring a highly specialized education from his mother.

"Amory."

"Yes, Beatrice." (Such a quaint name for his mother; she encouraged it.)

"Dear, *don't think* of getting out of bed yet. I've always suspected that early rising in early life makes one nervous. Clothilde is having your breakfast brought up."

"All right."

"I am feeling very old to-day, Amory," she would say, sighing, her face a rare portrait of emotion, her voice carefully controlled, her hands as poised as Sarah Bernhardt's 1 . "My nerves are on edge-- on edge. We must leave this terrifying place to-morrow and go searching for sunshine."

Amory's penetrating green eyes would look out   through his tangled hair at his mother. Even at this age he wasn't fooled by her.

"Amory."

"Oh, yes..."

"I want you to take a red-hot bath, as hot as you can bear it, and just relax your nerves. You can read in the tub if you wish."

She fed him the works of the Romantic Symbolists before he was ten; at eleven he could talk casually, if rather sentimentally, of Brahms and Mozart and Beethoven. One afternoon, when left alone in the hotel at Hot Springs, Amory sampled his mother's apricot cordial, and as the taste pleased him, he became quite tipsy. This was fun for a while, but then he spied a cigarette in his intoxication, and experienced a vulgar, common physical reaction to the drink and smoke. Though this incident horrified Beatrice, it also secretly amused her, and the story become part of her regular repertoire.

"This son of mine," he heard her tell a room full of awestruck, admiring women one day, "is entirely sophisticated and quite c harming--but delicate-- we're all delicate; *here* , you know." Her hand was radiantly outlined against her beautiful bosom; then sinking her voice to a whisper, she told them of the apricot cordial. They were highly amused, for she was a brave raconteuse 2 , but many keys were turned in sideboard locks that night against the possible sneakiness of the ladies' own devils.

[1] *Sarah Bernhardt was a famous French actress of this time.*

[2] *a female storyteller*

Describe the plot of this passage:

_____

_____

_____

What are the emotions, feelings, or personality involved in the passage?

_____

_____

_____

This passage is an introspective into the upbringing of both a mother and her son. The passage centers around a mother, Beatrice, who is well-educated and affluent. She has a child, Amory, who is also well-educated and peculiar. The passage delves into their interactions and personalities. They find great companionship in each other as Beatrice does not find that companionship with her husband and the father of Amory, Stephen.

What you would want to understand from this passage is that Beatrice is extremely affluent and well-traveled. She was educated around the world. She is passing that lifestyle down to her child, Amory, and their interactions are depicted as amusing and relaxed. He refers to his mother by her first name — Beatrice — rather than "mom." At one point, the young Amory takes a sip of alcohol and his mother uses it as an amusing story with her friends, where most parents might be livid at the idea of a ten-year-old taking a drink. This casual and peculiar relationship between the two characters would undoubtedly be the center of most of the questions. You could expect to see several questions about the characters' interactions, the nature of the relationships, and the personalities involved.

HISTORICAL PASSAGES

Many students find the historical passages to be the most challenging. The combination of dated vocabulary, complex sentence structure, and unfamiliar arguments makes the "old-timey" voice very difficult to interpret. All-too-often, students, anxious about not comprehending the passage's nuance, find themselves compelled to double-down on understanding *every* word. While certainly understandable, this mentality misses the fundamental difference between the SAT Reading and other forms of reading: on the SAT, **you only need to understand what will help you answer the questions!**

Don't try to understand each word — pay attention to the larger ideas. Most of the historical passages will articulate some form of argument, so focus on the topic that's being developed. For what is the speaker arguing? Why is this argument important? What's the speaker's tone?

Try applying these strategies by analyzing this brief fragment:

EXERCISE: HISTORICAL PASSAGE

I would be presumptuous, indeed, to present myself against the distinguished gentlemen to whom you have listened if this were a mere measuring of abilities; but this is not a contest between persons. The humblest citizen in all the land, when clad in the armor of a righteous cause, is stronger than all the hosts of error. I come to speak to you in defense of a cause as holy as the cause of liberty — the cause of humanity...

Ah, my friends, we say not one word against those who live upon the Atlantic Coast, but the hardy pioneers who have braved all the dangers of the wilderness, who have made the desert to blossom as the rose, the pioneers out West who rear their children near to Nature's heart, where they can mingle their voices with the voices of the birds-out there where they have erected schoolhouses for the education of their young, churches where they praise their Creator, and cemeteries where rest the ashes of their dead-these people, we say, are as deserving of the consideration of our party as any people in this country. It is for these that we speak. We do not come as aggressors. Our war is not a war of conquest; we are fighting in the defense of our homes, our families, and posterity. We have petitioned, and our petitions have been scorned; we have entreated, and our entreaties have been disregarded; we have begged, and they have mocked when our calamity came. We beg no longer; we entreat no more; we petition no more. We defy them!

You come to us and tell us that the great cities are in favor of the gold standard;1 we reply that the great cities rest upon our broad and fertile prairies. Burn down your cities and leave our farms, and your cities will spring up again as if by magic; but destroy our farms and the grass will grow in the streets of every city in the country.

Some have said that they fear a Robespierre.2 My friends, in this land of the free you need not fear that a tyrant will spring up from among the people.

What we need is someone who will stand against the encroachments of organized wealth.

Therefore, we care not upon what lines the battle is fought. If they say bimetallism3 is good, but that we cannot have it until other nations help us, we reply, that instead of having a gold standard because England has, we will restore bimetallism, and then let England have bimetallism because the United States has it. If they dare to come out in the open field and defend the gold standard as a good thing, we will fight them to the uttermost. Having behind us the producing masses of this nation and the world, supported by the commercial interests, the laboring interests and the toilers everywhere, we will answer their demand for a gold standard by saying to them: You shall not press down upon the brow of labor this crown of thorns, you shall not crucify mankind upon a cross of gold.

1 An antiquated financial practice where each dollar was matched with a certain quantity of gold.

2 During the French Revolution, Maximilien Robespierre executed thousands of wealthy French aristocrats and political dissidents.

3 Instead of using just gold, "bimetallism" calls for silver to also be matched to the dollar. This would devalue the dollar but make financial resources more accessible.

What is the author's tone?

_____

_____

_____

Describe the argument presented in the passage.

_____

_____

_____

On whose behalf is the argument made? Why, in the author's opinion, is this argument important?

_____

_____

_____

In this excerpt, you can see that the author argues for the replacement of the gold standard with what's called "bimetallism." You don't need to know what these policies are! You do, however, need to see how the author's argument develops. The author contrasts the "hardy pioneers" with the established merchants in the cities. The pioneers, the author asserts, are the backbone of the country, so any fair legislation must ensure their well-being. The author believes that he or she can "stand against the encroachments of organized wealth" and help the pioneers by abolishing the gold standard.

You can see how little of this analysis focused on the meaning of individual words. The first paragraph alone contains a slew of complicated vocabulary, so try not to get caught up in understanding everything. **Your background knowledge, too, might be misleading.** The SAT may sometimes try to trick you by presenting an unfamiliar argument from a familiar figure, or include answer choices with ideas that weren't explicitly in the passage. **<u>You'll be more likely to answer the questions correctly if you focus directly on the passage's broader tone and argument.</u>**

....

NONFICTION PASSAGES

As discussed earlier, there will be two types of nonfiction passages on the SAT: historical/social studies and natural sciences.

When reading nonfiction passages, you want to make sure to **identify the topic in the first few paragraphs.** Once you determine the passage's topic of the work, figure out what the **main point** is. Like in the historical passage, you'll want to try to analyze the author's tone and perspective. The author's perspective is the author's **point of view** - what the situation looks like from where the author is standing. This can be important to understand the author's **motivation** and **position** in the grand scheme of the passage. When there are multiple names mentioned in a passage, it is important to **keep track of who plays what role.**

For this next passage, try to pull out the **topic, main point, tone, and perspective.**

EXERCISE: PASSAGE UNDERSTANDING -NON- FICTION

Early Travel in the US

Prior to the advent of railroad transportation, people and goods traveled by animal-drawn wagons on turnpike roads. Beginning in the early 1800s, passenger travel to and from the ports and cities on both sides of the United States was accomplished by way of the National Road, a series of interconnected roadways linking major hubs. Later that same century, the Transcontinental Railway was constructed, which saved time and provided greater comfort during one's journey. Even so, travel was still a long way from being anything but a trying, exhausting experience.

The National Road's turnpikes were the 19th century equivalent of today's highways and stagecoaches were the equivalent of modern taxi cabs and buses. Together, they carried Americans across the country in the pre-railroad era. Stagecoach travel along bumpy, unpaved roads led some travelers to compare it to being "tossed in a blanket," with travelers often suffering head injuries from being thrown against the roof of the coach. Even short journeys over these roads left travelers physically exhausted and sometimes injured.

One traveler described his journey while crossing the Allegheny Mountains in 1847: "Our extensive vehicle had a significant inconvenience: it was impossible to lose sight of the absolute necessity for holding on. The great object was to prevent our heads coming in contact with the roof of the carriage, when any particularly violent jolt threw us with merciless force into the air…to be obliged to hold on with all our force to the seat, throughout the entire day, for fear of having our heads knocked in, was rather too much of a traveling inconvenience. We suffered nothing but great fatigue…I truly believe all the stories ofconcussion of the brain and other frightful misadventures connected with traveling across the mountains."

The kind of harrowing experience quoted here made the development of a quicker, more efficient, and less exhausting method of travel urgently necessary. Beginning in the 1860s, the US government funded the private construction of the Transcontinental Railroad, which would link smaller railroads in the east to the increasing number of towns cropping up in the central and western portions of the country. It took nearly a decade to complete. The fragmented construction saw many setbacks, including a great deal of corruption. It also saw the death of the many immigrants and freed slaves who provided the majority of the manual labor needed for such an enormous undertaking. However, the completion of the railroad was met with great excitement and enthusiasm by government officials and citizens alike.

Yet even as a considerably more efficient way to get from place to place, railroad travel s till posed some discomfort and inconvenience for its passengers as well challenges for railroad managers and staff. For a journey of more than a few hours, for instance, it was necessary to develop a plan for feeding the passengers. Doing this successfully was not as simple as it may sound. Some travelers carried their food with them, but a growing number were demanding meals along the road. "Eating houses" began to appear at junction points. These were privately owned establishments adjacent to train depots. But they were often mobbed with train passengers who had a too-brief window in which to purchase and consume a meal, meaning that many simply went hungry. It was not long before the railroads understood that it was in their best interest to make major improvements in the care and feeding of passengers. They also realized that delivering better food and more civilized service could produce extra revenue.

As transcontinental railroads took shape, the railroads increased their efforts to provide better meals, especially for those on extended journeys. By the late 1850s, travelers could book a trip from New Orleans to

New York on a combined river steamer and railroad route. The riverboats routinely provided sleeping and dining accommodations, so the railroads felt compelled to provide comparable service to customers who were accustomed to such luxuries. As train speeds increased more and more, it became impractical to stop for meals and the dining car was born.

After its slow start, dining on a train evolved into a more elegant and, at times even romantic, experience for early cross country travelers. During the "golden age" of railroading, from the 1890s through the 1920s, it was possible to eat a meal cooked by expert chefs and served by highly skilled waiters while being whisked across picturesque landscapes by a powerful steam locomotive.

Today, however, rail travel has naturally taken a backseat to air travel. Ever in search of greater efficiency and speed, the modern traveler can't, and won't, waste days doing what can be done in hours. One can still travel from New York to San Francisco by rail, but to do it comfortably can be crippling to one's wallet, while "budget" trips can soon make one regret the cramped seating, expensive microwaved food, and the lack of bathing facilities. All of which makes flying most people's first choice when booking travel arrangements today.

Topic _____

Main Point _____

_____

PAIRED PASSAGES

Paired passages are reading comprehension passages where there are two separate excerpts (usually surrounding the same or similar issue) and then a set of 10-11 questions. The first few questions are about passage A, the next few about passage B, and the final few concern both passages. **The best strategy is to read passage A first, then complete the passage A questions before reading passage B. Then read passage B and answer the remaining questions.** In doing this, you won't accidentally muddle the two passages together before answering the questions. By reading passage A and immediately answering the questions about it, you also **solidify the topic, main point, and tone** of passage A in your mind. You can then move on to analyze passage B and treat it as a new and distinct passage from passage A.

The trick here is that the passages can have varying relationships. Sometimes they are polar opposites — one is for something, one is against it. In other instances, the passages can be in partial agreement. Even more interesting is when the passages have very little relation other than the overarching topic. It is important to go into the dual passages **considering the relationship. It is not always pure disagreement,** which is what most students expect.

It is extremely important to contemplate the relationship between the two passages. The "dual" passage questions at the end of the question set will surely test you on your ability to understand the difference in opinion, or lack thereof, in the two passages. You will be required to understand the interplay between the two passages and how they work together. Aside from differences in stance, you want to consider how the passages present their information: **how do the authors make their points?** One passage may be more personal or philosophical, and the other more factual. What types of literary devices do they use? These can be crucial similarities or differences.

Try this exercise. Read these two passages carefully and determine the topic, main point, tone, and perspective for both passages. Think about how they work together.

Passage A

A selfie is a self-portrait taken with a smartphone. At least, that's what I assumed until two weeks ago when I stumbled on an article in *The Guardian* about the Getty Exhibition in Focus Play. "You do see self-portraits [in this photo-exhibition]," curator Arpad Kovacs said of the show, "but they are self-portraits. They are not selfies."

Instantly curious, I asked him to elaborate on the difference. He gave me a n interesting explanation. The self-portrait and selfie are two separate ways a person can create an image that defines himself. Sometimes these two ways of self-definition overlap, but not always.

Self-portraits were originally created by painters who carefully created their art. They chose the colors they used, the setting, and spent days or weeks composing the perfect portrait of who they believed themselves to be, or who they wanted to world to see them to be. A portrait is meant to be "read" as a work of art, to be studied and understood, and is intended to be a permanent record of an artist's effort.

But, to say that a portrait is permanent or "lasts" because it is better than a selfie is not necessarily correct. A portrait lasts because it was meant to. Selfies are created in a different context. Selfies are created in an instant; the actual creation happens in a push of a virtual button. A selfie is like a text; it is part of a conversation, intended to communicate an idea or a moment. As Arpad noted, "Selfies promote active discussion and responses that can be instantaneous and – more importantly – in the form of a selfie." Social media like Instagram exist so that people can converse almost entirely in images, largely selfies. These images are like text messages. Self-portraits, on the other hand, are documents. They are complex, multi-layered, and open to interpretation.

Selfies are meaningful in their social context. For example, a selfie of your best friend sitting in Starbucks is meaningful to you if you know that the cup in front of her is her favorite latte and that she's stopping there on her way to a job interview. To a stranger, she is just a woman with cup sitting in one of thousands of identical coffee shops. There is nothing to read in the image. A self-portrait, however, might be fraught with symbols and ideas embedded by the artist. A book on a shelf in the background of the portrait, for example, might tell the viewer, any viewer, that the sad smile on the subject's face comes from having just read a book of sonnets. An open window with a blowing curtain gives a hint of a spring breeze, and a tangle of flowers lying on table next to the subject suggests a rushed carelessness that begs interpretation.

To read selfies as self-portraits is to ignore their unique social purpose and in some cases to interpret them incorrectly. If, in your friend's Starbucks selfie, there happens to be a man in the background, should that person be interpreted or read as part of her image? Probably not. Selfies are not documents. Selfies may be art, but they are not necessarily self-portraits.

Passage B

The first thing you notice when you compare a modern selfie with a historic self-portrait is what is different about them. A self-portrait painting was created following a painstaking plan. The artist likely created many preliminary sketches. He viewed himself in mirrors over and over again, experimenting with different lighting and angles. Finally, he drew and painted his image, carefully choosing the right size canvas, the perfect colors, and the right brushes to have the perfect strokes. It was an expensive process that consumed weeks and months of his time. Selfies, on the other hand, are produced within seconds with a smartphone camera, and more often than not in poor lighting, with very little planning.

So, from the outset, the two methods don't seem to have much in common. But, when we step away from *how* these images are created, and start to think more about *why* they are created, or what is the purpose of these images, it seems like they are more similar than different. The important question to ask is not, what is an individual's purpose in creating an image of herself?

Essentially, both the self-portrait and the selfie are based on the idea or wish to freeze a slice of life. So, the purpose is the same, even if how the wish is executed is vastly different. The selfie is a spontaneous or spur-of-the-moment effort to freeze that moment, while the self-portrait is planned and considered. The qualities of the two images are different, but that doesn't mean that selfies are inferior to self-portraits. That means that they have different features or can be described in different ways.

Both selfies and self-portraits reveal something about the artists who created them. Both self-portrait artists and "selfie-artists" want to capture something special. They are trying to express something they feel inside for the outside world to see. They are sharing moods, feelings, and reactions to the world around them. It is a form of intuition, or intelligence of the unconscious.

Passage A

Topic   _____

Main Point   _____

_____

Tone   _____

Perspective   _____

Passage B

Topic _____

Main Point _____

_____

Tone _____

Perspective _____

How do these two passages relate?

_____

_____

What are the similarities and differences between the authors' opinions?

_____

_____

EXERCISE: HISTORICAL PAIRED PASSAGE

Sometimes, the historical passage may be offered as a paired passage. This is especially challenging, because students now have to place two historical texts in dialogue with each other. As you complete this historical paired passage, be sure to apply the both paired passage strategies and historical passage strategies.

Passage A

Friends and Fellow Citizens: I stand before you tonight under indictment for the alleged crime of having voted at the last presidential election, without having a lawful right to vote. It shall be my work this evening to prove to you that in thus voting, I not only committed no crime, but, instead, simply exercised my citizen's rights, guaranteed to me and all United States citizens by the National Constitution, beyond the power of any State to deny.

The preamble of the Federal Constitution says: "We, the people of the United States, in order to form a more perfect union, establish justice, insure domestic tranquility, provide for the common defense, promote the general welfare, and secure the blessings of liberty to ourselves and our posterity, do ordain and establish this Constitution for the United States of America."

It was we, the people; not we, the white male citizens; nor yet we, the male citizens; but we, the whole people, who formed the Union. And we formed it, not to give the blessings of liberty, but to secure them; not to the half of ourselves and the half of our posterity, but to the whole people--women as well as men. And it is a downright mockery to talk to women of their enjoyment of the blessings of liberty while they are denied the use of the only means of securing them provided by this Democratic-Republican government--the ballot.

For any State to make sex a qualification that must ever result in the disfranchisement of one entire half of the people is to pass a bill of attainder, or an ex post facto law, and is therefore a violation of the supreme law of the land. By it the blessings of liberty are for ever withheld from women and their female posterity. To them this government has no just powers derived from the consent of the governed. To them this government is not a democracy. It is not a republic. It is an odious aristocracy; a hateful oligarchy of sex; the most hateful aristocracy ever established on the face of the globe; an oligarchy of wealth, where the right govern the poor. An oligarchy of learning, where the educated govern the ignorant, or even an oligarchy of race, where the Saxon rules the African, might be endured; but this oligarchy of sex, which makes father, brothers, husband, sons, the oligarchs over the mother and sisters, the wife and daughters of every household--which ordains all men sovereigns, all women subjects, carries dissension, discord and rebellion into every home of the nation.

Passage B

The history of mankind is a history of repeated injuries and usurpations on the part of man toward woman, having in direct object the establishment of an absolute tyranny over her. To prove this, let facts be submitted to a candid world.

He has never permitted her to exercise her inalienable right to the elective franchise.

He has compelled her to submit to laws, in the formation of which she had no voice.

He has withheld from her rights.

Having deprived her of this first right of a citizen, the elective franchise, thereby leaving her without representation in the halls of legislation, he has oppressed her on all sides...

Now, in view of this entire disfranchisement of one-half the people of this country, their social and religious degradation -in view of the unjust laws above mentioned, and because women do feel themselves aggrieved, oppressed, and fraudulently deprived of their most sacred rights, we insist that they have immediate admission to all the rights and privileges which belong to them as citizens of the United States. The preamble of the Federal Constitution says: "We, the people of the United States, in order to form a more perfect union,

Passage A

Topic _____

Main Point _____

_____

Tone _____

Perspective _____

Passage B

Topic _____

Main Point _____

_____

Tone _____

Perspective _____

How do these two passages relate?

_____

_____

What are the similarities and differences between the authors' opinions?

_____

_____

FURTHER EXERCISES

Use these remaining passages to practice your skills. Read each passage looking for the topic, main point, tone, and perspective. If it is a fiction passage, make sure to pay attention to the emotion/feeling and plot. If it is a historical passage, don't get bogged down in the details — focus on the broader argument.

EXERCISE: FICTION

I My father's family name being Pirrip, and my Christian name Philip, my infant tongue could make of both names nothing longer or more explicit than Pip. So, I called myself Pip, and came to be called Pip.

I give Pirrip as my father's family name, on the authority of his tombstone and my sister — Mrs. Joe Gargery, who married the blacksmith. As I never saw my father or my mother, and never saw any likeness of either of them (for their days were long before the days of photographs), my first fancies regarding what they were like were unreasonably derived from their tombstones. The shape of the letters on my father's, gave me an odd idea that he was a square, stout, dark man, with curly black hair. From the character and turn of the inscription, "Also Georgiana Wife of the Above," I drew a childish conclusion that my mother was freckled and sickly. To five little stone rocks, each about a foot and a half long, which were arranged in a neat row beside their grave, and were sacred to the memory of five little brothers of mine — who gave up trying to get a living, exceedingly early in that universal struggle — I am indebted for a belief I religiously entertained that they had all been born on their backs with their hands in their trousers-pockets, and had never taken them out in this state of existence.

Ours was the marsh country, down by the river, within, as the river wound, twenty miles of the sea. My first most vivid and broad impression of the identity of things seems to me to have been gained on a memorable raw afternoon towards evening. At such a time I found out for certain that this bleak place overgrown with nettles was the churchyard; and that Philip Pirrip, late of this parish, and also Georgiana wife of the above, were dead and buried; and that Alexander, Bartholomew, Abraham, Tobias, and Roger, infant children of the aforesaid, were also dead and buried; and that the dark flat wilderness beyond the churchyard, intersected with dikes and mounds and gates, with scattered cattle feeding on it, was the marshes; and that the low leaden line beyond was the river; and that the distant savage lair from which the wind was rushing was the sea; and that the small bundle of shivers growing afraid of it all and beginning to cry, was Pip.

The marshes were just a long black horizontal line then, as I stopped to look back; and the river was just another horizontal line, not nearly so broad nor yet so black; and the sky was just a row of long angry red lines and dense black lines intermixed. On the edge of the river I could faintly make out the only two black things in all the prospect that seemed to be standing upright; one of these was the beacon by which the sailors steered—like an unhooped cask upon a pole—an ugly thing when you were near it; the other, a gibbet, with some chains hanging to it which had once held a pirate. A man was limping on towards this latter, as if he were the pirate come to life, and come down, and going back to hook himself up again. It gave me a terrible turn when I thought so; and as I saw the cattle lifting their heads to gaze after him, I wondered whether they thought so too. But now I was frightened again, and ran home without stopping.

Describe the plot of this passage:

_____

_____

_____

What are the emotions, feelings, or personality involved in the passage?

_____

_____

_____

....

EXERCISE: NATURAL SCIENCE

The forests of North America have seen plenty of change in a pretty short period of time, at least geologically speaking. Up until about 18,000 years ago, the Laurentide Ice Sheet covered Canada and much of the eastern United States. When temperatures climbed and the ice sheet retreated, forests gradually reemerged. But how? Did pockets of trees find refuge in sheltered areas during the Ice Age? Or were all tree species pushed to the southern tier of the United States, only to spread north again after the ice disappeared?

Scientists still debate the topic, but one thing is clear: today's forests in the eastern United States bear little resemblance to postglacial forests. Starting with European colonial settlers and marching through four centuries of development, drought, and fire, the tree cover of North America has become fragmented. "There are hardly any forests in the eastern U.S. that have never been cleared—maybe only a small percentage," said Claire Jantz, a researcher at the Woods Hole Research Center in Falmouth, Massachusetts. But changes in temperature, precipitation, and atmospheric concentrations of carbon dioxide could eventually do as much to remake the forests as humans did with saws and fires and bulldozers.

Jantz and her colleagues have been examining the state of current forest cover in National Parks, such the Appalachian region of the United States, while also modeling what the future of these forests will look like. They have been working in the Delaware Water Gap National Recreation Area (Pennsylvania and New Jersey), Shenandoah National Park (Virginia), and Great Smoky Mountains National Park (North Carolina and Tennessee). Jantz used the output from a large number of The forests of North America have seen plenty of change in a pretty short period of time, at least geologically speaking. Up until about 18,000 years ago, the Laurentide Ice Sheet covered Canada and much of the eastern United States. When temperatures climbed and the ice sheet retreated, forests gradually reemerged. But how? Did pockets of trees find refuge in sheltered areas during the Ice Age? Or were all tree species pushed to the southern tier of the United States, only to spread north again after the ice disappeared?

Scientists still debate the topic, but one thing is clear: today's forests in the eastern United States bear little resemblance to postglacial forests. Starting with European colonial settlers and marching through four centuries of development, drought, and fire, the tree cover of North America has become fragmented. "There are hardly any forests in the eastern U.S. that have never been cleared—maybe only a small percentage," said Claire Jantz, a researcher at the Woods Hole Research Center in Falmouth, Massachusetts. But changes in temperature, precipitation, and atmospheric concentrations of carbon dioxide could eventually do as much to remake the forests as humans did with saws and fires and bulldozers.

Jantz and her colleagues have been examining the state of current forest cover in National Parks, such the Appalachian region of the United States, while also modeling what the future of these forests will look like. They have been working in the Delaware Water Gap National Recreation Area (Pennsylvania and New Jersey), Shenandoah National Park (Virginia), and Great Smoky Mountains National Park (North Carolina and Tennessee). Jantz used the output from a large number of

1 *the arrangement of the natural and artificial physical features of an area*

Topic _____

Main Point _____

_____

EXERCISE: SOCIAL STUDIES

When it comes to economic choices, are people fundamentally rational or irrational? This ontological[1] question has given rise to two prevailing economic theories: traditional economics and behavioral economics. Traditional economics suggests that human beings make rational economic decisions, while behavioral economics assumes the opposite. It's important to recognize that "rational" and "irrational" in this case do not suggest that human beings are either fully logical or fully crazy, respectively. Traditional economics and behavioral economics are concerned with whether or not people tend to make objective, logical decisions.

Traditional economics makes three major assumptions. Firstly, it assumes that all people are rational; they possess and will always follow their sound, objective decision-making capabilities. Secondly, it expects people to always update their opinions correctly based on all available information. Finally, it believes that an individual will select the outcome with the most "subjective value" when presented with a choice. In other words, traditional economics expects people to allow their preferences to guide them into making the best logical decisions for themselves.

However, many economists suggest that these three assumptions cannot always be true. Studies from David Dunning, a renowned social psychologist, show that students consistently self-assess their competence to be higher than it actually is, with lower-performing students inflating their self-assessments the most. One could easily extrapolate how damaging this overconfidence could be for an investor deciding whether or not to invest in a struggling technological start-up. A plethora of psychological research shows that these kinds of biases underpin all forms of human decision-making. The fact that humans are unable to make objective assessments undermines the assumptions of traditional economics.

Many economists have embraced behavioral economics to address these more complex, irrational aspects of human behavior. Behavioral economics incorporates human biases into economic decisions. It also emphasizes how widely people's financial decisions are influenced by the context in which they make those decisions. Someone who recently lost his or her job, for instance, would be more likely to spend most of their savings on rent, food, and utilities when preserving their scant financial resources may be more advisable.

1 *Ontological inquiries attempt to discover the basic natures of a particular thing.*

Topic _____

Main Point _____

Tone _____

Perspective _____

SUMMARY

- Spend the time on the questions that are most likely to award you points.

- Understand the passage types and how they differ.

- Understand the time structure of the exam and how many minutes you have per question and per passage.

- Understand common question types (main purpose, vocab.-in-contect, detail extraction, paired-evidence, etc.)

- Prioritize the passages — do the "easiest" passage first.

- Make sure to read the introductory blurb at the top of the passage.

- Read the passage next, annotating wisely.

- Make sure to focus intensely on the introduction, conclusion, and first and last sentence of each paragraph.

- Make a roadmap of the passage while you read it.

- For Fiction passages, look for plot, character traits, and feelings/emotions.

- For nonfiction passages, look for topic, main point, tone, structure, and perspective.

- Take a moment after reading to digest the overall idea of the passage.

- Consider completing line reference questions first to build understanding.

- Consider completing "global" questions, like main idea questions, last.

- Pay close attention to the question stem and what the question is asking.

- Rely on the process of elimination.

- Nitpick words in the choices to eliminate statements that don't match the tone or style of the passage.

- For vocab-in-context questions, base your decision solely on how the word is being used in the situation (and not on its typical definition).

- Replace the vocab-in-context word with a synonym of your own choosing, then try to match it with a choice. As a last resort try substituting in answer choices.

- For main purpose questions, avoid specifics and pay close attention to words like "summary," "critique," and "analysis"

- Consider reading sentences before and after any line reference or vocab-in-context question

- Be detail-oriented when revisiting the passage for detail-extraction questions. Don't get fooled by bait language.

- Complete the paired-evidence questions simultaneously.

- For figure questions, pay attention to the title, axes, and units. Relate the information presented in the figure to the passage's overall argument.

- For paired passages, reading Passage A and then immediately answer the Passage A questions. Then move on to Passage B and the remaining questions.

- Do not draw your own conclusions. Find some level of evidence (even if it's not direct) to support your answers. Reasonable inferences should not require connecting too many dots.

- Make sure you keep an eye on the clock throughout the section. Do not wait until you are on the last passage to check your time.

SAT WRITING & LANGUAGE

....

WHAT'S THE GIST?

The Writing & Language section is the second portion of the exam. You will have **35 minutes** to complete **44 questions**. This section is split into four passages, each containing 11 questions.

Each question is a multiple choice question with 4 possible answer choices. Not every problem will appear with a physical question; you might simply be provided with 4 possible corrections to an underlined portion of the text. Many questions will contain a "NO CHANGE" option, which allows you to keep the language in the original text unchanged.

WHAT CAN YOU EXPECT TO SEE?

The questions on the exam will fall under two major categories: usage & mechanics and rhetorical writing skills. The first tests your ability to follow the rules of standard English. The second tests your ability to edit writing so that it is clear, purposeful, and organized.

USAGE AND MECHANICS:

Conventions of Standard English:

- Punctuation (commas, colons, semicolons, possessive apostrophes, dashes, and parentheses)
- Sentence Structure (parallelism, proper modifiers, identifying/fixing run-ons, fragments, comma splices, and weak conjunctions, etc.)
- Proper verb tense and subject/verb agreement
- Pronoun agreement

RHETORICAL WRITING SKILLS:

Knowledge of Language:

- Deleting redundant and wordy language
- Choosing language consistent with style and tone
- Revising unclear writing
- Word choice and idioms

Organization, Unity, and Cohesion:

- Selecting proper transition words/phrases
- Rearranging sentences/paragraphs
- Combining two sentences
- Selecting effective opening or closing statements for a paragraph/passage

Topic Development (Purposeful and Focused Writing):

- Determining relevance of information to the focus of a paragraph/passage (adding/deleting sentences or phrases)
- Selecting a word/phrase/sentence to accomplish a specific task
- Interpreting figures/graphs and relating the information to the passage

STRATEGIES

First things first, **go in order and answer the questions as you read**. This is the one section of the exam where it does not make sense to skip around. The passages and questions are of the same difficulty and style, so it's best to just go in order.

That being said, there are a f**ew types of questions that you may not want to answer right away.** You may get a question, for example, that asks you to select a good introduction or transition sentence. That's really not possible to answer unless you have a good idea of what you're trying to introduce or transition into. So you should read on, determine what the main idea is, and then answer the question accordingly.

Next, **you don't want to focus solely on the underlined portions of the sentence**. First, you may miss a bigger error in the overall sentence structure if you narrow your focus on one particular part of the sentence. What may sound fine as a snippet may be problematic for the sentence as a whole. Sentence structure is a widely tested topic, so it's important that you read sentences (and your proposed corrections) **in their entirety.** We will discuss the specifics of sentence structure later on, but know that you should be mindful of this concept at all times.

> Ex: The professor <u>who researched the flight patterns of Canadian geese</u>, who become flightless for several weeks during the summer months, using advanced tracking devices.

> The phrase "the professor who researched the flight patterns of Canadian geese" doesn't necessarily register as wrong. There's no improper verb tense, pronoun usage, or punctuation-nothing that your ear will identify as being problematic. When we read the full sentence, however, we realize that there's an issue in the overall sentence structure. We have a subject (the professor), but there is no *active* verb in the sentence. The phrase "who researched the flight patterns of Canadian geese" is <u>simply describing the subject</u>. There's nothing telling us what the subject is *doing*. That would be like saying: "The car that was parked outside….." You'd think "what *about* the car parked outside?!"

Issues with sentence structure will sometimes require us to add more language; other times, it will require us to remove language. You should always think:

1) **Do I have enough?**
2) **Do I have too much?**

Again, we discuss sentence structure in greater detail later.

Sometimes, the SAT will get <u>really</u> tricky and give you a mistake to fix **in hopes that you ignore a potentially bigger one.** Let's say they *had* used an incorrect pronoun or verb tense. Your mind thinks it's spotted the error, fixes it, and then moves on. But you still have to **make sure that the correction works for the entire sentence and that there are no bigger issues that need fixing.**

Be sure you **identify *specifically* what is being underlined and what language the answer choices *actually* contain.** The SAT will try to trick you by assuming that you'll carelessly identify what is being corrected and not reevaluate your correction in context. .

Ex: The human resource department collected <u>more then a</u> handful of resumes from the local job fair.

The main issue here is clear; "then" should be replaced with "than." That doesn't mean you should circle the first answer you see that contains "than." You might see answer choices like these:

a) NO CHANGE

b) more than

c) at least a

d) several

You might default to selecting (b) based on what you assumed your correction would entail. You would be wrong to select it. This answer choice does not contain the "a," which was included in the underlined portion of the original sentence. Anything that's underlined is up for deletion; if it belongs in the sentence – like the "a" in our example – you need to be sure that you pick an answer choice that includes it.

Reread the sentence with your correction to double check that it makes sense contextually and grammatically. Hearing it in your head (and even mouthing the words) will really help you to identify if something is missing.

Before we move on, let's take one more look at the previous example.

Ex: The human resource department collected <u>more then a</u> handful of resumes from the local job fair.

a) NO CHANGE

b) more than

c) at least a

d) several

If you hadn't noticed the issue with answer choice (b), you may have found yourself struggling to decide between answers (b) and (c). They both effectively illustrate the same idea in about the same number of words, so they both appear right. **That should be a red flag! We cannot have two correct answers**, so if you find that you're deciding between two "right" answer choices, you've probably missed a problem with one of the answer choices. It's also very possible that they are **<u>both</u>** incorrect, which leads us to our next strategy.

Eliminate answer choices that are essentially the same. Certain words or forms or punctuation are essentially **identical**. Sure, they are *technically* different, but they serve the exact same purpose. You will never be asked to choose stylistically between two correct options. They can't both be right, so that means they're both wrong!

The **semicolon** and the **period** are identical (at least for the purpose of the SAT). If one answer choice contains a period and the other a semicolon, and **everything else about the answer choices is the same, <u>eliminate them both immediately.</u>**

Transition words/phrases that are synonyms of one another should also be eliminated:

- Thus = Hence = Therefore = As a result = Consequently
- However = Conversely = Contrastingly
- Nevertheless = Regardless
- Additionally = Furthermore
- Similarly = Likewise

....

For our next strategy, let's revisit one of our earlier examples.

> Ex: The professor <u>who researched the flight patterns of Canadian geese,</u> who become flightless for several weeks during the summer months, using advanced tracking devices.

Our goal here is to **simplify longer/difficult sentences**. When we first talked about this example, we compared it to the statement "the car that was parked outside." It was easy to identify a mistake in the second example because it was so short. The sentences on the exam are going to be longer and more involved, so we want to look for ways that we can simplify them so that our ear can more easily identify possible mistakes.

Lifting out any non-essential information is a great place to start. Phrases that lie in between parentheses, double dashes, or double commas (although you should note that not all language between two commas is removable) are not necessary and can be removed from the sentence. We'll talk about that more when we do our punctuation lesson. If we removed the extra information enclosed between the commas from the example above, the sentence becomes much easier to absorb. It would read as:

> Ex: The professor who researched the flight patterns of Canadian geese using advanced tracking devices.

Here are some things you can do to simplify longer/difficult sentences

- **Reword longer phrases.** Instead of "scientists from Columbia University's advanced geology department and researchers from NASA's aerospace training division," rephrase the statement as "group A and group B."

- **Remove unnecessary information.** That includes non-essential, descriptive information (like we saw in the example above), dependent clauses, and transitional words
- **Replace difficult or fancy language** with words you're more familiar with. If you recognize a word or phrase, but it's not something you would use in everyday language, replace it with language you would regularly use.

....

Lastly, **don't forget about the bigger picture.** Writing needs to be grammatically correct, but it also needs to be purposeful. The whole point of language is conveying meaning to illustrate an idea, so you want to pick words, phrases, and entire sentences that **emphasize the main idea being discussed.** That's another reason why we don't want to focus solely on the underlined portions of sentences or even just on the sentences that contain possible corrections. There are going to be plenty of sentences that are not subject to corrections, but you should still be reading them! If you don't, you'll miss out on a lot of contextual information. You don't need to read *too* carefully, but you'll want to know what the overall point, structure, and tone of the passage are.

This is especially helpful for questions that ask us to conclude a passage. To answer this effectively, you have to know what the passage is about. You won't have that understanding if you ignore entire pieces of writing. If you are still a little unsure about what the passage's main idea is, don't reread the entire thing: **reread the title, briefly skim through the intro/conclusion, and read the topic and closing sentences of each paragraph.** This will give you a pretty good idea of what the passage was about and help you select a proper conclusion.

....

Now that we have a better idea of how to tackle the English section as a whole, let's discuss some strategies for specific types of questions, namely those dealing with punctuation, verb tense, and sentence structure. These are topics we will be reviewing in greater depth later on. If you feel these are weak areas for you, you may want to skip ahead to review these concepts before focusing on the strategies.

For starters, **know your rules for punctuation**. There are a lot of questions you can rely on your ear for, but punctuation shouldn't be one of them. Instincts aren't enough, so make sure you really solidify the actual rules of punctuation.

This is especially important for commas. For the purpose of the SAT, there are 5 major reasons for using a comma. Those reasons should guide your comma usage. It can be tempting to say "I would take a natural pause when saying this sentence, so I must need a comma," but you should only use a comma when there is a legitimate purpose for it. Placing it into one of those five categories will help you determine if a comma is legitimately usable or not. You don't want to get fooled into placing punctuation where it doesn't belong. Even if there's a lot of text, that doesn't mean a comma is necessary. Generally, **less is more when it comes to commas** on the exam.

This is another reason why simplifying sentences is useful. Earlier, we talked about shortening phrases like "scientists from Columbia University's advanced geology department and researchers from NASA's aerospace training division" into "group A and group B." We mostly did that so that the sentence was mentally easier to digest, but it's also a good technique for comma placement. If we wouldn't put a comma between "group A and group B," we don't need one in the longer example, even though it contains significantly more language.

We also spoke about lifting out non-essential information as a means of simplifying longer sentences; this has a direct relationship to comma usage. Additional information commas are often seen in pairs for the purpose of <u>interjecting extra information into the middle of a sentence</u>. The extra information is not necessary for grammar, sentence structure, or context. **If we're ever unsure if we have a situation that calls for the double commas, we can lift out the information between the commas and see if the sentence still makes sense.** If the sentence does not require the information in question, we will surround the language with double commas.

Again, we will discuss in detail the rules for commas and all forms of punctuation later on. Make sure to review those rules and refer back to them on the exam. The SAT recognizes the most common misconceptions with punctuation rules and fills the exam with traps. If you know the rules very well, you're less likely to fall for these tricks.

....

Let's talk about one grammar concept that you *can* rely on your ear for: subject verb agreement. Errors in subject-verb agreement don't happen often in everyday speech, so they're pretty easy to spot. You wouldn't say "the book are heavy" or "the boys loves going skiing." The problem is, once again, that you will be dealing with much longer and trickier sentences. The SAT will use that to its advantage; it will place a lot of language between the subject and the verb so that your ear is less likely to pick up on any mistakes.

Luckily, there's a simple fix: **identify the subject and read it directly next to the active verb.** The subject is the specific noun performing the action in the sentence, or having the action happen to it. It is **NOT** always the noun that appears just before the verb. It's typically one of the earlier nouns in a sentence.

> Ex: The exercise demonstrated by the skilled instructors, who each worked as chiropractors for the surrounding communities, <u>were difficult</u> to master.

> The verb in question here is "were." To determine if this is the proper tense, we need to find our subject. There are several nouns in the sentence that can easily throw us off track, but the actual subject is "the exercise." If we read the subject directly next to the active verb, we will spot the error immediately. "The exercise were difficult" is clearly not correct.

> The sentence contained several plural nouns before the verb "were" that trick the ear into thinking there are no issues. Carefully identifying which noun was the actual subject completing the action was crucial.

Questions dealing with subject-verb agreement can make excellent use of our next strategy: **when in doubt, pick the answer that is the least like the other three.** You might be familiar with the jingle **"One of these things is not like the others."** That sort of thinking may help you when all else fails. For verb tense questions, if three answer choices line up with a singular verb, and only one lines up with a plural verb, it's likely that the unique choice is the correct one.

SINGULAR SUBJECT (she, the book, etc.)	PLURAL SUBJECT (they, the cars, etc.)
is	are
was	were
has	have
Verb that ends in "s"	Verb that does NOT end in "s"

Circling back to our example, here are some choices you may have seen.

Ex: The exercise demonstrated by the skilled instructors, who each worked as chiropractors for the surrounding communities, <u>were difficult</u> to master.

a) NO CHANGE

b) have been difficult

c) was difficult

d) are difficult

Answers (a), (b), and (d) would all work for a PLURAL subject. The verbs "were" and "are" and the helping verb "have" would all pair with a plural subject. The verb "was" is the only option that would pair with a SINGULAR subject. That is our correct answer choice; it pairs with the subject of the sentence: the exercise.

If you had misidentified the subject and assumed it was the "instructors" or "communities" that needed to be paired with the verb, you may have thought to yourself that "were difficult," "are difficult," and even "have been difficult" all sounded fine. **Remember, that should be a red flag! We can't have two (or three) correct answers!** Do not just circle the one that you "like" the best.

....

Many of the questions on the SAT don't have much to do with grammar rules at all, but rather deal with the notion of **clear, concise, non-redundant and purposeful writing**. These questions test your ability to <u>edit</u> writing so that it is effective in building an overall argument. This may seem subjective, but **the SAT will have its own set of rules to apply to writing.** Once you become familiar with these "rules," identifying the correct answer will become much simpler.

Let's start with one of the most important rules of all: **concise is nice. <u>Very often, the shortest answer choice is the most effective.</u>** If more language is required to provide clarity, a relevant detail, or proper grammar, a longer answer choice might be necessary. For example, we can't use a short pronoun like "it" if it's not clear what "it" is referring to, so sometimes more language is necessary. But if it's **clear** what's being said and the sentence is structurally sound, **the SAT will always favor something with fewer words.**

It's not just wordiness that shorter answers help to fix. Shorter answer choices will also indicate that you may need to search for r**edundancies. If one answer choice is significantly shorter than the rest (or the exam gives you the option to delete/omit language), you want to search carefully for redundancies.** <u>If information has already been stated, you don't need it.</u> The redundant information isn't always nearby. Sometimes the repeated information is a detail that was given sentences or even paragraphs away. Don't get tricked into thinking that repetitive information is necessary for emphasis. Remember to think about the "rules" for the SAT: they will always favor the choice that relays the necessary information as concisely as possible.

> Ex: In 1849, Monterey – located on the coastline of Central California – became the state's first official capital. Several diplomats from the surrounding areas met <u>in the mid 1800's in</u> Monterey to sign California's first constitution after months of careful consideration and discussions.
>
> a) NO CHANGE
> b) in the coastal city of
> c) following lengthy deliberations in
> d) DELETE the underlined portion

All of these answer choices are grammatically correct and we were not presented with a question that asked us to include a specific *type of detail*. That means an argument can be made for more than one of these answers, which is a problem!

But there is a bigger issue with these answer choices, and choice (d) gives us a big clue as to what that problem is: redundancies. The phrase "in the mid 1800's," although informative, is completely unnecessary. The preceding sentence already specified that this event took place in 1849. The phrase "in the coastal city of" is also repeating information found in the preceding sentence. The phrase "following lengthy deliberations" is essentially rephrasing the language found later in the sentence, which specifies that the event occured after months of discussions. Although none of these phrases were *identical* to the information found nearby, they are all illustrating points that have already been made and thus are unnecessary.

Several questions will ask that you effectively combine two sentences. You are typically given control over the two sentences *in their entirety*. While there isn't a concrete approach for these problems, the main goal is to **maintain the <u>meaning</u> and <u>relationship</u> between the original sentences**. We also want to be sure we are conveying that message **clearly** and **concisely**. Keep the following in mind:

- **Do NOT add unnecessary/new language.** While we may swap out some words/phrases with synonyms that are *slightly* longer (like "also" with "in addition"), we are not adding *unnecessary* words or entirely new information/language.

- **Do NOT eliminate/change <u>important</u> language.** While we may want to eliminate *unnecessary* language (like a repeating subject) for the purpose of making our sentence **concise**, we don't want to eliminate language that is crucial to our understanding of the sentences or **<u>how they relate to one another.</u>** A word like "by," as small as it is, has major implications. It creates a cause and effect relationship between our two sentences. We wouldn't want to eliminate it or swap it out for another word that changes the initial relationship of the sentences.

  Ex: The number of donations grew at an unprecedented rate. This growth caused the charity's newly designed website to crash.

  Here, we can remove the unnecessary language by restructuring the second statement:

  > The number of donations grew at an unprecedented rate, causing the charity's newly designed website to crash.

  What we would **NOT** want to do is eliminate any language that minimizes the cause and effect relationship of the original statements like we see here:

  > The number of donations grew at an unprecedented rate, and the charity's newly designed website crashed.

- **Do NOT rearrange language without cause.** Several answer choices will start to rearrange the language in a way that makes the statement unclear and/or gramatically incorrect. We don't want to lose clarity by rearranging the language *without cause*. The only reason to restructure language is to **place descriptive phrases as close to the thing(s) being described as possible.**

  Ex: Advocates of the proposed economic policy were passionately debating the topic with hesitant party leaders. The policy supported massive tax cuts for small businesses.

  In this case, it makes sense to rearrange the language for the purpose of clarity and conciseness. The second sentence simply describes the policy mentioned in the first sentence. We can reword it slightly and place the description right after the policy is first introduced:

  > Advocates of the proposed economic policy, which supported massive tax cuts for small businesses, were passionately debating the topic with hesitant party leaders.

This may seem like a lot to consider for a single problem, and it is. But ultimately your job is to look for a combination that **does not change much of the original statements**. Sometimes it's as simple as swapping out the period for a colon or a semicolon. Remember that you'll also want to consider **clarity** and **conciseness** in the same way you would any other question on the writing and language section.

....

The next few strategies will all deal with word choice and idioms. Word choice problems will require you to select <u>the most appropriate term for a given situation</u>. You will need to select the word with the correct meaning/spelling and the one that matches the author's tone.

Unfortunately, some of these questions will come down to luck. You may not recognize all of the possible words or know which spelling is accurate. Selecting between cite and site, allusion and illusion, and conscious and conscience are a few examples that have appeared on exams, but they are nearly impossible to prepare for. Memorizing hundreds of vocabulary words is not an effective way to prepare, so we will simply need to rely on some other skills and memorize the meanings/spellings of the words that DO appear regularly. These include:

- Then vs. than
- Affect vs. effect
- Fewer vs. less

Note: We will discuss these all in greater detail later.

Generally, **you will want to avoid casual or conversational language** and pick phrases that are more formal. If you have the choice between "a bunch of" and "several," you should absolutely select "several."

It's also crucial that you **know the difference between informal speech and written grammar.** <u>The way we speak and the way we write are different</u>, so you can't rely strictly on how something *sounds*. One of the most common mistakes occurs with the phrases "would have," "could have," and "should have." When spoken, most will use the contraction "would've," which *sounds* a whole lot like "would *of*." The latter is <u>completely incorrect</u>, which is proof that we cannot rely solely on our ears for questions of this nature.

Do not default to selecting a word *just* because it's familiar to you. If your instinct tells you it doesn't belong in the specific sentence, use that as a reason to eliminate it. It's safer to select an unknown word than a word with which you are familiar with that you're certain doesn't work for the given situation.

> Ex: The measuring devices were deemed ineffective. After a follow-up study was performed, it was determined that the original findings were <u>deceitful</u>.

a) NO CHANGE

b) erroneous

c) insincere

d) wacky

We'll make use of a couple of the strategies we have discussed so far. The first answer choice we can eliminate is "wacky," as it is far too informal/conversational. Contextual clues from the sentence before and the underlying pattern in our answer choices help us understand that the sentence is trying to indicate that the findings were **wrong**.

We must be picky with our answer choices, however. Words like "deceitful" and "insincere" are both typically used to characterize a *person*, and they both indicate that the errors were *intentional*. This situation does not call for that. So we are left to pick a word that we may not have recognized, but that's okay! We can make a solid argument against the other choices, so it's a pretty safe bet to choose "erroneous," which means false.

Minor differences in the answer choices are incredibly important for questions like these. **Some words can be used as synonyms in certain situations, but not in others**. Words like "wrong" and "unethical" can be used interchangeably if we are discussing actions that are immoral or corrupt. We can call a politician's decision to lie to the public "wrong" or "unethical." However, we can't use both of these words in *all* situations. We can say that the statement "2 + 2= 5" is "wrong," but we wouldn't be able to say it is "unethical." When it comes to word choice, it will always come down to the specific situation, and that's what must be considered.

....

Idiom-based questions, like vocabulary questions, will sometimes come down to luck in the sense that you may or may not recognize the given phrase. Idioms are peculiar phrases in English that culturally develop over time but wouldn't make much sense to you if English wasn't your native language. A phrase like "cold feet," for example, indicates that someone is nervous; it does not mean that their actual feet are chilly! Don't worry too much about questions like these. They will never account for too many questions on a single exam and it does not make sense to attempt memorizing dozens of idioms.

....

One type of word choice problem that *will* account for several questions and that we *can* prepare for are transitional words. **Transition words/phrases** – ones like "however," "additionally," "for example," "nevertheless" – are an important topic on the SAT. These words help to emphasize some sort of relationship between two thoughts, often between a sentence and the sentence before or after. To select a proper transition word, you must **determine what that relationship is.** Follow these steps:

1) Reread the sentence before and/or after and paraphrase what it's about

2) Reread the sentence containing the question **without the transition word already provided.** The transition word that's already there is not correct, which will tend to warp

your idea of what's being said. Reading the sentence without the current word/phrase gives you a clean slate. Paraphrase what this sentence is about.

3) Determine what type of relationship exists between these two statements. There are a handful of relationships that you might run into, but the most common are the following:

    a) Cause and effect

    b) Contrast

    c) Addition

    d) Similarity

    e) Illustration

4) If it's difficult to determine which type of relationship you have (and by extension, what word/phrase to select), rely on some of your basic test taking strategies. **Eliminate synonyms and/or any answer choices that you are certain do NOT work** for this situation.

Let's discuss the common relationships in greater detail.

Cause and Effect: when the second statement is a **result** of the first. Common transition words/phrases for this relationship are:

- As a result
- Thus
- Hence
- Therefore
- Consequently (this does NOT have a negative connotation)

Contrast: when two **strikingly different** thoughts are presented next to each other. Common transition words/phrases for this relationship are:

- However
- Conversely
- In contrast
- On the other hand (often following "on one hand")
- Whereas
- Despite
- Nevertheless
- Regardless
- Even so

    Note: Some of these have *slightly* different meanings.

Addition: when new information is presented to reinforce an idea. Common transition words/phrases for this relationship are:

- Additionally
- Furthermore
- Moreover
- Also

Similarity: when <u>closely related</u> ideas are used to express agreement or emphasize an idea. Common transition words/phrases for this relationship are:

- Similarly
- Likewise

Illustration: when specific details/instances are used to support the preceding statement. Common transition words/phrases for this relationship are:

- For example
- For instance
- Namely

Some less common relationships you may also run into:

Summary (to wrap up or rephrase an idea): in short, in other words, in summary
Order (to define some element of time/chronology): Lastly, finally, firstly, then
Emphasis (to indicate importance): indeed, in fact

Be detail-oriented when it comes to selecting transitional words. Illustration, addition, and similarity are all relationships that agree with or continue an argument, so they can be difficult to differentiate.

Ex: Following the hurricane that devastated the coastal cities, several cases of looting and home break-ins were being reported. <u>However,</u> instances of assault and other violent crimes saw a surge in the aftermath of the storm.

a) NO CHANGE
b) For example,
c) Conversely,
d) Additionally

Let's work through our steps:

1) The first sentence is discussing the increase in crimes (robbery related) following a hurricane.

2) The second sentence is discussing the increase in violent crimes following the hurricane.

3) The second sentence is providing extra information that ties into the discussion begun in the first sentence. For that reason, "additionally" is a great option.

4) If we weren't convinced that "additionally" is the proper choice, we could start eliminating the incorrect/repetitive options. "Conversely" and "however" are synonyms of one another, so we can eliminate them both. They also don't make any sense in this context given that there is no contrast between the two statements. "For example" also does not make sense for this situation. Although our sentences are working together to support an argument, the second statement is NOT an example of what was discussed in the first sentence.

Our correct answer, then, is "additionally."

It's possible that none of the transition words will apply to the situation you're given; in that case, you'll have the option of not including any transition words. That's perfectly fine! Do not feel forced into selecting a transition that doesn't belong.

. . . .

Let's now discuss rhetorical writing skills on a larger scale. These types of questions will not require you to select the proper grammar, but rather the proper *content*. Once again, you will be forced to consider the bigger picture and edit the text so that it is **clear and purposeful**. You may see questions that require you to:

1) Edit entire sentences or phrases

2) Order or place sentences or paragraphs

3) Delete or add possible sentences or phrases

4) Interpret graphs/figures and pair it with the passage's claim

Let's start with the most important strategy of all: **pay attention to the question**! Several problems on the writing and language section don't appear with actual questions, but **if there *is* a physical question, read it <u>carefully</u> and <u>circle the key words</u>**. All of the answer choices are going to be grammatically correct and somewhat relevant, but you want to select the answer choice that <u>satisfies whatever conditions they've given you</u>.

If you are asked for the most descriptive sentence, choose the one with the most descriptive language. If you are asked for the sentence with the most specific detail, choose an answer choice with stronger, more precise language. We can't rely on eliminating answer choices that are "incorrect" in the grammatical sense, so you have to pay close attention to what it is the question asks you to do.

Ex: The teacher reviewed the paper <u>for several minutes</u> before determining that the student had plagiarized a portion of the essay.

Which choice most specifically emphasizes the extreme extent to which the teacher reviewed the document?

a) NO CHANGE

b) intensely

c) for some time

d) with painstaking detail for almost an hour

The phrases we should be paying close attention to in the question are "specifically emphasizes," and "extreme extent." With those in mind, it is clear that answer choice (d) is our best option. While the other answer choices were grammatically correct and/or dealt with *part* of the question prompt, only this answer choice gives us the most <u>specific details</u> (indicating it was almost an hour and not merely "several minutes" or "some time") and <u>bold language</u> that highlights the effort level of the teacher (with the phrase "painstaking detail"). An answer choice like "intensely" does illustrate some level of extremity, but does not contain any specific details.

Note: You may have been tempted to select choice (b) because it is the most concise. While we generally favor more concise answers, the briefest answer did not properly address the question in this circumstance. It was more important that we satisfy the condition presented to us in the question first.

If you come across a content question like this and you are completely stuck, **choose the one that is the least like the other 3**. It's possible that because the answer choice deviates in some way from all the others that it is the only one that actually answers the question.

....

You will often be asked to select/edit entire sentences, very often either introductions, conclusions, or transitions. We touched on this briefly when we were discussing some more general strategies, but let's discuss this in greater detail. As a reminder, **we cannot answer these questions without reading the surrounding information**.

- For **introductions**, we will want to read ahead, determine what the paragraph's main idea is, and select a statement that relates to that information.
- For **conclusions**, we will want to reread the paragraph before, determine its main idea, and select a statement that wraps up that discussion
    - If asked to conclude the **entire passage** , determine the passage's <u>main idea</u> by rereading the title, introduction, and first and last line of each paragraph

- For **transitions**, we will want to skim <u>both the paragraph before **and** after</u>, determine the main idea of each, and select a statement that bridges those two ideas together.

Ex:

    With a matter of weeks until the election, Senator Myers was doing all that she could to boost her approval ratings. She attended several national events for veterans and underprivileged communities, and helped to raise funds for a number of highly regarded charities.

    <u>The vote was scheduled to take place on September 15th, just weeks before her 55th birthday.</u> Voters found her to be unauthentic and opportunistic. Focus groups described her philanthropic endeavors as "mere photo ops that lacked true empathy or compassion for the American people." Uncertain that they would be able to regain momentum, Meyer's campaign manager resigned unexpectedly.

Given all the answers are true, pick the one that provides the most effective transition.

    a) NO CHANGE

    b) Meyers grew up in Oregon, where she would be finishing up the final days of her campaign tour.

    c) Despite these efforts, the American people were not impressed.

    d) Some of the charities she worked with included the National Alliance to End Homelessness and The Global Fund for Women.

To select a proper transition, the sentence should somehow bridge the gap between the information that came before it and the information that follows. It's also crucial that **any** sentence addition (transitional or otherwise) contains information **relevant at <u>this</u> point in the passage.** Information that is loosely related to the subject is never correct. While answer choices (a) and (b) both provide information about Meyers and/or the election, they are not pinpointing the main ideas of these two paragraphs.

The first paragraph talks about Meyer's efforts to gain approval with the population through various means. The next paragraph goes on to discuss the issues she encountered. While answer choice (d) focuses on what information came before (by further describing the involvement in charities), it does nothing to introduce the information that follows. Answer choice (c) perfectly connects the two paragraphs by referencing the efforts discussed in the previous paragraph and then highlighting the problems discussed in the following sentences.

....

A handful of questions may require you to pull information from graphs or figures that accompany the passage. Your job is to **read the figures carefully** and to **pay close attention to what the question is asking.** This is still a content-based question. Like any other content question, it's not enough to pick a true statement. We have to think about what the question is asking and select the choice best satisfies that specific condition.

Ex:

A study conducted in 2003 determined which methods of transportation were most used among workers and non-workers in 9 major American cities. Students were considered unemployed citizens for the purpose of this study. Private automobiles, public buses, and trains/subways were the most frequently used. Cycling, walking, and car services constituted a majority of the "other" modes of transportation. Compared to unemployed citizens, <u>employed citizens are much more likely to ride the train or subway</u>.

Preferred Transportation Methods of Employed and
Unemployed Citizens from a 2003 Survey

	Private Automobiles	Bus	Train or Subway	Other
Employed Citizens	36%	11%	32%	21%
Unemployed Citizens	19%	28%	31%	22%

Which choice provides an accurate interpretation of the chart and logically concludes the sentence?

    a) NO CHANGE

    b) employed citizens are significantly less likely to use the bus

    c) employed citizens spend significantly more time traveling in a private automobile

    d) 32% of employed citizens take the train or subway

To answer this question effectively, we need to read the table *carefully*. It's not enough to extract numbers from the table: what do those numbers *actually* represent? We also must consider the question prompt, which is asking us to logically conclude the sentence provided.

Choice (d) is a true statement but does not logically conclude the sentence. The sentence is structured to form a comparison between unemployed and employed citizens. Choice (d) does not draw a comparison between the two groups, so we should eliminate it. Choice (a) is not supported by the graph. It claims that employed citizens are <u>much more likely</u> than unemployed citizens to ride the train, but the percentages are nearly the same. The employed group has a *slightly* higher value listed, but the difference is not enough to warrant such a strong statement. Choice (c) is tempting at first glance, but when we look at that answer choice more closely, it will fall apart. The graph displays the amount of people that prefer each mode of transportation; it does not give us any information about how much *time* is spent traveling. That leaves us with choice (b), which is both effective in concluding the sentence and supported by the graph.

Another content-based question you will encounter are sentence addition/deletion questions. For these, you will be asked whether or not a phrase or entire sentence should be included in the passage. There are two major things to keep in mind for questions like these: relevance and flow. Sentences should be added/kept when they:

- Provide relevant detail for the argument being made at this point in the passage
- Provide explanatory or clarifying information not found elsewhere (remember, we don't like redundancy)
- Do not disrupt the conversation

Relevance can be tricky here; it's not enough that the information be relevant to the passage as a whole. **It must be relevant at this specific point in the passage**. Read a few sentences before and after the potential line addition, determine what is being discussed, and decide whether or not this information would **help to build towards the argument**. That means it can't be <u>loosely</u> relevant. Providing a random fact, even if it has some connection to the information in the paragraph, is not necessary. **The information has to emphasize the main point.** If it does, we will keep/insert it.

If the text in question does not provide something of significant relevance or it **disrupts the flow of the paragraph**, we will delete/omit it. Interrupting the current discussion is just as problematic as being irrelevant.

Thinking about *purpose and order* should help you decide whether a statement belongs, but that's only half the battle. Each answer choice will also contain a justification to support your decision. **Read the justifications carefully and in their entirety.** It can be easy to only focus on the "yes/no" part of the question and skim through the justifications, but that will very often get you into trouble. Several of the justifications are wholly or partly untrue.

The good news is you can use that to your advantage! If you're having difficulty determining whether or not something should be added or deleted, focus on the justifications and eliminate the ones that are wrong.

After some practice, you will start to recognize the type of language that is often found in the proper justifications. Many times when we delete something, it's because the statement distracts the reader or blurs the focus of the paragraph, so you will see words like "blurs," "disrupts," and "distracts" in the justifications. Again, make sure the justifications are *entirely* true; many of them are designed to trick you. It's not enough to say the sentence is a distraction; be precise with the language. What *exactly* is it a distraction from?

Ex:

The chances of a diagnosis were slim [1]. Specialists from around the world were called upon to provide any insights they may have, but doctors still struggled to find a solution.

The author is considering adding the following statement at point [1]. Should they make this addition?

,with fewer than .05% of the hospital's cases reporting similar symptoms.

a) Yes, because it explains the procedure doctors use to make proper diagnoses.

b) Yes, because it specifically illustrates why the diagnosis was difficult and emphasizes how dire the situation was

c) No, because it does not adequately explain which type of specialists were contacted.

d) No, because it undermines the central claim of the paragraph

The given information provides <u>specific details that are relevant to the argument being</u> <u>made</u>. For this reason, the addition should be made. That narrows it down to choices (a) and (b), but it's important that we now properly determine **precisely** what the information tells us. It does not explain in any way *how* diagnoses are made, so answer choice (a) can be eliminated.

You could also arrive at the correct answer by focusing on the justifications. We have already discussed why the justification for (a) is not accurate. Answer (c) uses a justification that does not make any logical sense, as the sentence in question is not focused on the specialists. Answer (d) claims that the statement undermines the central argument, which is not true. To undermine something means to weaken the argument, and if anything, this phrase helps to *support* the argument even further. That would leave us with (b) by default.

Ex:

The hurricane devastated much of the Louisiana Coast and left local legislators scrambling for solutions. Local councilwoman Laura Mackey was one of the first to organize a massive collection and distribution of supplies. [1] Everything from canned goods to blankets to toilet paper was donated on behalf of the families in need. A second councilmember organized the creation of more than a dozen pop-up hospitals to care for the injured.

The author is considering adding the following statement at point [1]. Should they make this addition?

Mackey first ran for city council in 2005, just five years after finishing law school.

a) Yes, because it describes how Mackey was able to organize the collection of supplies

b) Yes, because it provides specific details about Mackey's qualifications and how she used those skills in the post-hurricane efforts

c) No, because it distracts the reader from the paragraph's focus on Mackey's career achievements.

d) No, because it is only loosely tied to the paragraph's focus on legislators' responses to the natural disaster.

The phrase in question is tied to the paragraph in some way, but to what extent? We don't want to include new information if it's *loosely* related to the information in the paragraph, which is exactly what we have here. The phrase provides extra information about Laura Mackey, but that is not the main focus of the paragraph. The paragraph discusses the aftermath of the hurricane and how local government stepped in to provide relief. Further discussion about Mackey's personal or professional life would not add anything to the overall argument.

Now that we know it doesn't belong, we have to read the justifications carefully. Choice (c) sounds great at the beginning; the word "distracts" is particularly tempting. But when we read the remainder of the answer, the justification falls apart. The paragraph is not about Mackey's career achievements. Recognizing that the proposed addition was a distraction is only half the battle; we need to figure out more specifically what it distracts *from*. Answer choice (d) does that more accurately by identifying the government's response to the disaster as the main idea of the paragraph.

Any addition at this point in the paragraph would also disrupt the current conversation. The line before introduces the collection and redistribution of supplies. The next line gives more precise information about which supplies were donated. These lines belong next to each other.

If you weren't certain whether or not the phrase belonged, you could have relied on eliminating the incorrect justifications. We already determined that the justification for (c) was inaccurate, and we can do the same for choices (a) and (b). The addition in no way describes *how* the supplies were collected/distributed, as choice (a) implies. It also doesn't describe how Mackey used any of her learned skills in her hurricane efforts, as choice (b) implies. We were simply given some background information about Mackey's early career.

....

Let's move on to sentence placement and ordering. You may be asked to determine where in a paragraph or where in the passage a statement should be added. For these questions, **try to establish a relationship between the sentence and another sentence in the paragraph/passage.** Direct references, transition words, or some element of time can help place a sentence.

- If the sentence opens with a phrase like "These studies proved…," we need to place this sentence **after** those specific studies have been introduced.

- If a statement starts with a transition word, we need to place it near a thought that relates to the statement in question through the relationship established by the transition word. For instance, if the statement begins with a transition word like "however," we need to place it *after* a sentence that would *contrast* with that statement.

If we don't have an obvious link to another sentence in the paragraph (or passage), you will simply want to place the statement based on what makes sense chronologically. You also want to be sure that we are **not being disruptive**. We spoke earlier about avoiding disruptions to existing conversations; that same concept should be applied to these questions.

Ex.

[1] Jericho's county fair was attracting thousands of tourists from the neighboring counties. [2] Citizens came pouring into Jericho to play games, enjoy locally sourced food, and take a ride on what local newspapers called "the Ferris wheel to end all Ferris wheels." [3] Taking these figures into account, city council members decided to add a second fair later in the year. [4] Standing 350 feet high, the Ferris wheel could be spotted for miles, welcoming travelers from all directions. [5] The fair's total revenue was estimated at 1.2 million dollars, bringing a much needed boost to the local economy.

For the sake of logic and cohesion, sentence [3] should be placed:

a) Where it is now

b) Before sentence 1

c) After sentence 4

d) After sentence 5

You may have recognized that sentence 3 felt out of place when you first read through the paragraph. For starters, it is disrupting the conversation about the Ferris wheel; sentence 2 should lead right into sentence 4.

Sentence 3 also contains a direct reference to something: the figures. That means this sentence should be placed after figures have been introduced, which occurs in sentence 5. So we will place sentence 3 after sentence 5.

....

Before we move onto the rules for punctuation, grammar, and sentence structure, let's wrap up our discussion of Writing & Language strategies by revisiting one of our general test-taking strategies: **categorizing the questions.** Determining what concept is at the root of each question helps you figure out exactly what to look for in the answer choices and what potential traps to avoid. It's usually pretty easy to identify when a question is dealing with punctuation, verb tense, or word choice based on the answer choices. Questions that appear with physical question prompts (sentence placement, sentence addition/deletion, author intent, ect.) are also easy to categorize.

As we discussed earlier, we can generally assume that wordiness and/or redundancy is being tested when one answer choice is significantly shorter than the rest or we're given the option to delete language. When it's not quite obvious what's going on, it's probably an issue of sentence structure. There is a section in our upcoming English review that deals with all of the possible issues with sentence structure (parallelism, misplaced modifiers, run-ons, comma splices, fragments). You should pay close attention to all of these structural elements when you believe that sentence structure is the root of the problem.

COMMAS

It can be tempting to try and use your instincts for comma questions by "hearing" where natural pauses in a sentence may occur. You'll want to rely more on the actual rules for commas so that you are not tricked into adding commas where they don't belong. A large amount of text does not always call for a comma, so it is important to know the specific reasons why commas are utilized. Here are the 5 major reasons:

1) Joining two independent clauses WITH a coordinating conjunction

In other words, when you have two complete sentences and want to combine them with a "connecting" word.

- The acronym FANBOYS may help you remember the possible coordinating conjunctions: For, And, Nor, But, Or, Yet, So

    Ex: The student could spend his time reading, but he would rather be playing video games. ✓

"The student could spend his time reading" and "He would rather be playing video games" are both complete sentences, so the comma used **with** the conjunction "but" is necessary to combine the two clauses.

Note: Sometimes the SAT will combine two independent clauses with a comma but NOT include a coordinating conjunction. Do not fall for their tricks! This is called a **comma splice** and is grammatically incorrect. You need a comma **AND** a coordinating conjunction.

    Ex: David went to the store, he purchased many items. ✗

This is INCORRECT as there is no coordinating conjunction between the two independent statements.

2) Separating nouns/actions in a list or multiple non-essential modifiers

This is probably the type of comma you are the most comfortable and familiar with. We use it to separate multiple items, actions, or phrases.

    Ex: My three favorite fruits are apples, bananas, and strawberries. ✓

    Ex: Maria is going to clean her room, do her laundry, and finish her homework. ✓

We also use it to separate multiple non-essential modifiers. It's important to distinguish between essential and non-essential identifiers. **If you can change the order of the adjectives, they are non-essential and will require commas.**

      Ex: Sophie was a brave, enthusiastic patient. ✓

Here, "brave" and "enthusiastic" are interchangeable and therefore **non-essential**. The sentence would still make sense if it was written as: Sophie was an enthusiastic, brave patient.

In some sentences, descriptive words or phrases are **essential** and belong next to the noun.

      Ex: Julia was asked to read over Dylan's detailed history notes. ✓

Here, "history" is describing the TYPE of notes and "detailed" is our non-essential adjective. It would not make sense to write it as: Julia was asked to read over Dylan's history detailed notes. So we do not need a comma.

....

You can also **use the "and" trick** to help you with questions of this nature. **If you can place an "and" in between your descriptive words, you will need a comma.**

      Ex: Sophie was a brave and enthusiastic patient. ✓

      Sophie was a brave, enthusiastic patient. ✓

Note: We do NOT need a comma after the final adjective. We only add commas BETWEEN our adjectives.

      Ex: Sophie was a brave, enthusiastic, patient. ✗

Remember, **less is more when it comes to commas.** This is especially true for these types of comma questions.

3) Transition words or phrases

Selecting the proper transition word or phrase is something we have already discussed, but now it's important we understand how to punctuate them. Commas are needed to separate these words from the rest of the sentence, whether they appear at either the beginning, end, or middle of a sentence.

If they appear at the beginning of a sentence, we use a comma after the word or phrase. If they appear at the end of a sentence, we use a comma before the word or phrase.

      Ex: However, many of the students did not complete the assignment. ✓

Ex: Many of the students did not complete the assignment, however. ✓

If they appear in the middle of a sentence, we "hug" the transition word/phrase with double commas.

Ex: The students, however, were unwilling to accept the amount of work that had been assigned to them. ✓

4) Opening a sentence with a dependent clause

Let's start by discussing what a dependent clause is. A dependent clause is simply something that can't stand alone. It **depends** on an independent clause to make sense. Many times, dependent clauses will contain subordinating conjunctions like "while," "during," "since," or other indications that the information relies on another statement to make sense.

"While Jessica was reading" cannot stand alone. Even though "Jessica was reading" is a complete sentence, the "while" requires us to have more information for the sentence to actually mean anything. That information is the **independent clause**, which can appear at the beginning or end of the overall sentence. **If the independent clause appears at the beginning and is followed by the dependent clause, we don't require any punctuation.**

Ex: Nicholas was watching television while Jessica was reading. ✓

If we restructure the sentence so that the dependent clause comes <u>FIRST</u>, we need to separate the dependent clause and independent clause with a comma.

Ex: While Jessica was reading, Nicholas was watching television. ✓

Not all dependent clauses will contain those subordinating conjunctions, but it will be clear that the statements cannot stand on their own.

Ex: Fearful of roller coasters, Emily rejected David's invitation to go to Six Flags. ✓

5) Additional information

Commas are used to add **non-essential** phrases or clauses to a sentence. This can be done two ways: in the middle of a sentence or at the beginning/end of a sentence.

When the additional information is added to the end of a sentence, we simply add a comma before the non-essential phrase. When the additional information is added at the beginning of a sentence, we simply add a comma after the non-essential phrase.

Ex: Tourists flocked to the newly constructed stadium, located just north of the expressway. ✓

When the information is **interjected** into the **middle** of a sentence, we "hug" that information with double commas. It is easy to tell when we have this scenario because **we can remove that information** and the sentence will still make sense and be grammatically correct.

> Ex: The stadium, located just north of the expressway, was attracting hundreds of tourists per week. ✓

If we removed the phrase "located just north of the expressway," the sentence would read as: The stadium was attracting hundreds of tourists per week. Because this statement is grammatically correct and understandable, we know the additional information can be enclosed by the double commas.

Note: This process of figuring out whether information is essential or not (and whether or not commas are needed as a result) is especially difficult with names. Remember to ask yourself whether or not you NEED the name for the sentence to make sense.

> Ex: Astronaut Neil Armstrong was the first man to walk on the moon. ✓

Here, Neil Armstrong's name is **necessary** to understand the sentence. As it is essential, we **do not section it off with commas**.

> Ex: An astronaut, Bethenny Samstein, visited the high school to discuss space camp with the student body. ✓

Here, the name of the astronaut is **not necessary** grammatically or contextually. Because it is non-essential, we **surround the name with the double commas.**

....

DASHES AND PARENTHESES

Dashes and parentheses are both used to insert additional/explanatory information into a sentence.

Dashes can be used in a very similar way that commas are used to insert additional information, in that they can be **used in pairs** to interject a statement into the **middle** of a sentence or **alone** at the **end** of a sentence.

The main difference between dashes and commas is that the information between the dashes is often more abrupt. It can disrupt the flow of the original sentence. Sometimes the statement between the dashes is its own sentence!

> Ex: She read so slowly—English was her second language—that her teacher suggested she hire a tutor. ✓

Just like the double commas, **we can remove the information** between the dashes and the sentence will make sense.

We can also use a single dash at the end of a sentence to provide extra information.

Ex: The woman demanded two things from her children—appreciation and respect. ✓

The SAT will never make you choose stylistically between dashes and commas. They **will** try to trick you into selecting answer choices that contain one comma and one dash, which is **NOT** correct. You will hug additional information with either TWO commas or TWO dashes, never a mixture of the two!

....

Parentheses are used to enclose explanatory information. The SAT will mostly test you on **where** a parenthetical statement belongs. Your job is to place this information directly after the thing it is describing.

Ex: Scientists discovered several new celestial objects using a government funded telescope and an advanced data processing system (natural objects located outside Earth's atmosphere). **✗**

This is **NOT** a correct use of the parentheses. The information enclosed is meant to define a celestial object, so it should be placed directly after that term.

Ex: Scientists discovered several new celestial objects (natural objects located outside Earth's atmosphere) using a government funded telescope and an advanced data processing system. ✓

....

SEMICOLONS

Semicolons are sometimes referred to as a "weak period." Grammatically, **they do the same thing that** periods do: separate two independent sentences. A semicolon is used when the two thoughts are very closely related, but the SAT will never make you decide stylistically between semicolons and periods.

Remember, that means if you see them both, you can eliminate them both! They can't both be right!

If you're not sure if a semicolon belongs in a sentence, read it with a period and see if both sentences can stand on their own.

Ex: Maria wasn't sure what she should bring to the picnic; eventually, she decided to bring brownies. ✓

Here, the semicolon is perfectly fine because it is separating two independent clauses and a period could have easily been put in its place.

Ex: Carlos was certain he wanted to bring chips to the picnic; because they are his favorite snack. ✗

Here, the semicolon is **NOT** used properly. "Because they are his favorite snack" is not a complete sentence, so we cannot use a semicolon.

....

COLONS

Colons are very simply used to introduce related information **after a complete sentence**. It is very important that what comes **before** the colon be an **independent clause**, but what comes **after** the colon can take **many** forms. Don't be fooled into thinking that lists are the only thing that can follow a colon! As long as the information provides some sort of detail or information related to the opening statement, it can be anything: a list, a word, a name, a phrase, a quote, or even another complete sentence.

Ex: I need to purchase several ingredients to bake an apple pie: sugar, flour, and apples. ✓

Here, the three items placed after the colon specify the ingredients referenced in the opening sentence. What the colon essentially did here was **eliminate the need for language like "which are."**

Don't be fooled into picking an answer choice that contains language like "which are" or "such as" AND a colon.

Ex: I have three favorite hobbies: which are skiing, dancing and swimming. ✗

This is **NOT** correct.

....

Colons are **not always followed by a list!** Sometimes the information will be very short and succinct, but other times the information will be lengthy, and that's okay. Don't shy away from a colon just because what follows it is a longer phrase or complete sentence.

Ex: Jared loved the artistry in the performance: each dancer was more ornately dressed than the last. ✓

Here, the statement following the colon is a complete sentence, but as it provides specific information about the preceding statement, a colon is perfectly acceptable. The phrase **before** the colon was a complete sentence, and that is really the most important thing.

....

POSSESSIVE APOSTROPHES

Possessive apostrophes, as their name suggests, are meant to indicate possession or ownership.

For **SINGULAR** nouns, you will add the apostrophe **BEFORE** the "s."

> Ex: That car's tires are flat. ✓

Because I am referencing a single car (as indicated by the word "that"), the apostrophe is placed before the "s"

For **PLURAL** nouns, you will add the apostrophe **AFTER** the "s."

> Ex: Those cars' horns are very loud. ✓

Here, I am referencing multiple cars (as indicated by the word "those"), so the apostrophe is placed after the "s."

Sometimes it will be obvious whether a noun is singular or plural based on its spelling. The word "baby," for example, changes its spelling to "babies" when it is made plural. For a word like "car," the spelling does not change so you will have to **use contextual clues** from the sentence or passage to figure out if you are talking about one or several cars.

VERBS

When it comes to verbs, the SAT is mostly concerned with two things: **correct tense** and **subject-verb agreement.** Let's begin with verb tense. This is one concept that you can rely pretty heavily on your ear for. Verb tense is generally not something we mess up in everyday speech, so errors are fairly easy to spot.

If we want to get technical, there are six basic tenses:

> **Simple present:** They swim.
> **Present perfect:** The have swum.
>
> **Simple past:** They swam.
> **Past perfect:** They had swum.
>
> **Simple future:** They will swim.
> **Future perfect:** They will have swum.

Some of these tenses can be a little tricky, especially with a word like "swim," whose past tense requires more than simply adding "ed" to the end of the word.

For all the **perfect** tenses, we use what is called the **past participle**, in this case "swum." We also need to use helping words like "have/had" for the perfect tenses. Sometimes the SAT will try to trick you into choosing an incorrect version of these trickier tenses.

> Ex: They have chose to see a Broadway musical. ✗

This is **NOT** correct. The verb in question here is "choose." "Chose" is its simple past tense and "chosen" is its past participle. We would not mix a simple past tense with the helping word "have." Proper sentence structures could include:

They chose to see a Broadway musical.

They have chosen to see a Broadway musical.

They had chosen to see a Broadway musical.

....

Figuring out which tense to use also comes down to context. You must figure out what tense the author is writing in to select the correct verbs. Looking for other verbs in the sentence and other verbs in the preceding sentences can give you some important clues about the proper tense. **In most cases, we rely heavily on consistency.**

Ex: The teacher explained to the student that he can visit her office hours at any time and that she will be happy to help him. ✗

This sentence is **NOT** correct because it mixes the past tense (explained) with the present tense (can) and future tense (will be).

Ex: The teacher explained to the student that he *could* visit her office hours at any time and that she *would* be happy to help him. ✓

Note: In some cases, it DOES make sense to have multiple tenses in one sentence. You'll just need to use your instincts to ensure it makes sense.

Ex: I was invited to attend the school dance, but I think I will be vacationing that day. ✓

Here, we have several different tenses in one sentence, but the progression from past to present to future makes sense in this context.

Ex: Next summer, I was swamped with school work. ✗

Here, the reference to the future ("next summer") combined with an activity in the present perfect tense ("I was swamped with school work") makes no sense.

....

One of the most commonly tested topics dealing with grammar usage is **subject-verb agreement.**

The basic concept is:

If your subject is **SINGULAR**, the verb will **END WITH AN "S".**
If your subject is **PLURAL**, the verb will **NOT END WITH AN "S".**

It is very easy to hear mistakes when this rule is broken!

Ex: The girl walk to the store. ✗

Ex: The boys walks to the store. ✗

Refer back to the strategy section to locate important skills for tackling these questions. These questions can be rather tricky, as the SAT will place distractor subjects ahead of the verb to trick your ear into believing that an incorrect subject-verb pairing is correct. Avoid those traps by solidifying those strategies.

....

PRONOUNS

Pronouns are words that we use in place of a noun or noun phrase. These are words like you, he, her, them, it, those, who, which, etc.

For the most part, your job will be making sure the pronouns **match** the nouns they are referring to and that they are **clear**. It is totally unnecessary to repeat a noun several times within one sentence (or even multiple sentences) if it is **clear** what is being referenced.

> Ex: Sally is very interested in space, so she applied for an internship at NASA. ✓

> Ex: Working at NASA had always been a dream of Sally's. She applied for an internship in the engineering program as soon as she was old enough. ✓

In both cases, the pronoun "she" is close enough to "Sally" for the reader to understand what is happening. If the noun is stated at the end of the preceding sentence, we very rarely need to start the following sentence with restatement of the noun (as you can see in the second example above.)

"She" also matches with "Sally," because Sally is a singular female noun. Make sure you figure out what noun is being described by the pronoun and that the two match. Think about:

Singular vs. plural (he vs. they)
Male vs. female (he vs. she)
Active vs. passive (he vs. him)
Human vs. object (he vs. it)

....

Pronouns that do not match the noun or do not clearly indicate who/what is being talked about are incorrect.

> Ex: Paul was fighting with Steven, so he decided not to go to his birthday party. ✗

It is totally unclear who "he" and "his" are referring to, so this sentence needs clarification. Even though the SAT loves concise answer choices, sometimes the lengthier option is necessary for this purpose.

> Ex: In a rush to get out of the house, Cynthia left their keys on the kitchen counter. ✗

Here, the plural pronoun "their" does not match with "Cynthia," so this sentence is incorrect.

> Ex: Each student on campus is given a detailed itinerary describing the events they are required to attend. ✗

This one is exceptionally tricky. As reader, we understand that there are multiple students who are given itineraries, so the phrase "they are" does not strike us as incorrect. The sentence is structured, however, with the subject being "each student." This is singular, so we would use a phrase like "he or she is."

> Ex: Each student on campus is given a detailed itinerary describing the events he or she is required to attend. ✓

....

Be careful with "her" vs. "she." Pronouns like "I," "he," "she," "they," and "we" belong with **active** verbs. These pronouns are actually **completing the action.**

Pronouns like "me," "her," "him," "them," and "us" are **passive**. These pronouns are **having the action done *to* them.**

> Ex: **She** threw the ball to **him**. ✓

This is obvious, but thinking about active/passive pronouns can help you when things get a bit more difficult.

> Ex: The parents had dozens of questions for Nicholas and I. ✗

"I" is not the correct pronoun here. Even though the phrase "Nicholas and I" generally sounds okay, it is incorrect in this case because those two nouns are **passive**. Think of how you would answer the question: Who did the parents have dozens of questions for?

We would respond with a "me" and not an "I," so we will use "me" in the original statement.

....

This idea of active/passive also helps greatly when choosing between **who** and **whom**. "Who" is used in the active sense and "whom" in the passive sense. If you rephrase the statement as a question, would you answer with "he/she/they" or a "him/her/them"? If it's the first, use "who." If it's the latter, use "whom."

> Ex: Sarah, **who** threw the ball to David, was being blinded by the sun.
> Who threw the ball to David? **She** did.

> Ex: David, to **whom** Sarah threw the ball, was being blinded by the sun.
> Who did Sarah throw the ball to? She threw it to **him**.

....

Pronouns like "who," "that," "which," and "whom" are usually used to introduce some additional information about a particular noun. Again, make sure they match. "Who/whom" are used to describe people and "that/which" are used to describe things and animals.

Ex: The scientists, which were all recent graduates of the mechanical engineering program, were working tirelessly to solve the ongoing crisis. ✗

Here, the wrong pronoun is used to further describe the scientists. Given that scientists are human beings, we would use the term "who" instead of "which."

....

Possessive pronouns are used to indicate ownership. Instead of adding an apostrophe (like we do with standard nouns), we use words like "my," "his," "its," "their," and "whose." The two most difficult – and the ones you will be tested on the most frequently – are "its" and "their."

Let's begin with "its." You will see three forms of this word on the exam.

1) Its
2) It's
3) Its'

The first (**its**) is used for **possession**.

Ex: The cat was adorable. Its tail was striped and fluffy.

The second (**it's**) is the **contraction** of the words "it is."

Ex: Make sure you wear gloves. It's very cold outside.

The third (**its'**) is a completely made up word! **Never pick it!**

Moving on to "their." You will see three forms of this word on the exam.

1) Their
2) There
3) They're

The first (**their**) indicates **possession**.

Ex. The cats were adorable. Their tails were striped and fluffy.

The second (**there**) can be used to indicate **location** or to **open a sentence.**

Ex. The books are located over there.

Ex. There are several options for diners to select from.

The third (**they're**) is the **contraction** of the words "they are."

> Ex. Be careful around raccoons. They're aggressive and territorial animals.

....

Before you worry about which form of "its" or "their" to use, you must FIRST determine which pronoun ("it" or "they") works for the given situation. "It" is used for singular subjects; "they" is used for plural subjects. The SAT loves to lay out traps with these types of questions.

> Ex: The students voted to select <u>it's</u> new class pet. ✗

Certainly "it's" is not correct: "it is" class pet makes no sense. But changing the word to "its" gives us another problem: **a mismatching pronoun**. The subject of the sentence is the students. That is a plural subject, so "it" (and by extension, the possessive form "its") will **not match**. We would need to change the word to "their," which indicates possession **AND** matches with our subject.

....

WORD CHOICE AND IDIOMS

Word choice problems will require you to select the most appropriate term from a given situation. You will need to choose the option with the correct spelling/meaning and one that matches the author's tone. **Consult the strategy section to review the important skills necessary to approach these questions.** Right now, we will be reviewing the rules for some of the most common word-based questions.

Then vs. Than: "Then" is used to denote some element of time. "Than" is used when we are drawing a comparison.

> Ex: She planned on visiting her mother and then going to the store. ✓

> Ex: The student was smarter than her teacher. ✓

Affect vs. Effect: "Affect" is the verb (think "a" for action). "Effect" is the noun (think "e" for event).

> Ex: The ongoing effects from the hurricane crippled the local economy. ✓

> Ex: The vote was greatly affected by the previous night's presidential debate. ✓

Fewer vs. Less: Both of these words are meant to indicate a smaller amount of something. Figuring out which one to use comes down to what you are comparing. If it's something that is **countable**, use "fewer." If it is something that is **measured** or a **characteristic** of something, use "less."

> Ex: I have fewer friends than you do. ✓

Ex: I have less friends than you do. ✗

The second example doesn't necessarily strike us as incorrect, so if the question is dealing with less vs. fewer, **think actively about the rule, and don't rely entirely on your ear.**

Ex: I am less skilled than my mentor. ✓

Ex: It rained much less this month than it did last month. ✓

....

As a reminder, **idioms** are peculiar phrases in English that you may or may not be familiar with. The SAT will typically test you on verb-preposition pairs like the ones listed below:

Ex: The odds are **IN** your favor

Ex: Please refrain **FROM**

Ex: She alluded **TO**

....

Would/Could Have vs. Would/Could of

A reminder that "would of" is **NOT** proper English! "**Would have**" is very often shortened to "would've" which merely *sounds* like "would **of**."

Don't get fooled into selecting answer choices based solely on how they sound when you read them allowed. Like just now! "Allowed" is not the right term. It *sounds* the same as "aloud," but has a totally different meaning from the correct word for this situation. Look out for these traps.

....

Into Which, From Which

This is one of the more challenging question types, because you probably don't structure sentences this way when you write. Let's start with an example first.

Ex: The driveway **she drove into** was freshly painted. ✓

Ex: The driveway **into which she drove** was freshly painted. ✓

Typically we place words like "from" or "into" **after** a verb. But we can structure the sentence in such a way that these words come **BEFORE** the verb. We need to use words like "which" or "whom" in these cases. It may feel a little unnatural at first, but don't eliminate it as an option just because it's a bit unfamiliar. Many of the other answer choices they will provide will not contain a necessary "into" or "from" term **ANYWHERE** in the sentence. That is definitely **worse** than placing it in a spot that you don't prefer.

Ex: The author from whom I drew my greatest inspiration was Edgar Allan Poe. ✓

....

ADJECTIVES AND ADVERBS

Another concept you may see tested on the SAT is the use of adjectives and adverbs (typically in pairs). This is something you may be able to rely a bit on your ear for, but if we want to get technical:

Adjectives – modify nouns

Adverbs – modify verbs, adjectives, and other adverbs

Adverbs typically end in "ly" or "ily." The important thing is to pair an adverb and adjective in the correct order and to not mistakenly use an adverb as an adjective. Again, this will probably sound wrong to you when you hear it being misused, so you can rely a bit on your instincts.

Ex: The baker had an exceptionally precise way of measuring ingredients. ✓

"Precise" is the adjective describing the form of measurement and "exceptionally" is the adverb modifying "precise."

Ex: The baker had an exceptional precisely way of measuring ingredients. ✗

This sentence is not properly structured, placing an adjective in front of the adverb.

....

Adverbs do not need to be paired with adjectives, but it is important that they not come directly before a noun.

Ex: The burglar creepily walked down the hallway. ✓

Here, the adverb is simply modifying the verb "walked."

Ex: The amazingly performance kept audience members at the edge of their seats. ✗

Here, "amazingly" is incorrectly attempting to modify the noun "performance." If we want to indicate that the performance is amazing, we simply use the adjective "amazing."

....

COMPARISONS

Comparisons can be a bit tricky when we compare a noun to something found later in the sentence. We must make sure the comparison is **complete and logical.**

> Ex: The experienced actor's level of professionalism was rivaled by the young actress hoping to make a name for herself. ✗

This sentence may not sound wrong initially, but it is. We must break it down and figure out *specifically* what we are comparing. We are not comparing the actor to the actress; we are comparing the actor's *level of professionalism* to the actress's *level of professionalism*. As the sentence is right now, we are essentially comparing a level of professionalism directly to a person. When we really think about it, that doesn't make sense! It would be wordy and unnecessary to repeat "level of professionalism," so we can use a pronoun.

> Ex: The experienced actor's level of professionalism was rivaled by **that of** the young actress hoping to make a name for herself. ✓

Make sure you choose a pronoun that matches what you are actually comparing. In this example, "level of professionalism" is single and non-human, so the pronoun "that" is sufficient in setting up the comparison.

SENTENCE STRUCTURE

Before we discuss the potential issues with sentence structure, let's first review the makings of a complete sentence. A complete sentence requires two things: a **subject** and a **verb**. The sentence must also be a **complete thought**, which will often require additional language (like an object).

The **subject** of the sentence is the noun that is **doing** or **being** something.

The **verb** is the **action being performed** or the **state of being**.

For problem sentences, you will not always be given control over the punctuation, so you may need to alter the **language** so that it follows the rules of punctuation and grammar. You may remember from the strategy section that you should be asking yourself two things:

1) Do I have enough?
2) Do I have too much?

How to deal with either of those issues will come down to which portion of the sentence is underlined (and thereby under your control) and what your answer choices are. You may have to change/add proper punctuation, delete language, or add language.

....

COMMA SPLICES

You may recall that a **comma splice** occurs when two independent clauses are incorrectly connected with **JUST** a comma (and **no coordinating conjunction**). We can fix this problem by transforming one independent clause into a dependent clause or modifying statement. We do this by <u>removing the subject and/or active verb</u>.

> Ex: She grew up on a farm, she was not afraid to pet the horses. ✗

> Ex: Having grown up on a farm, she was not afraid to pet the horses. ✓

Here, we changed the <u>opening statement</u> from a complete sentence into a modifying statement about our subject.

> Ex: She sat in hours of traffic, this made her late to dinner. ✗

> Ex: She sat in hours of traffic, making her late to dinner. ✓

Here, we changed the structure of the <u>closing statement</u> to eliminate the issue of the comma splice.

....

RUN-ONS

Run-ons are created when two independent sentences are connected <u>by nothing at all</u>. Again, we will need to add, eliminate, or edit the language to avoid the error in sentence structure.

> Ex: The gingerbread cookies were fresh out of the oven they filled the house with smells of Christmas. ✗

There is often more than one way to fix an error. We just need to make sure that we don't end up creating another problem.

> Ex: The gingerbread cookies were fresh out of the oven and filled the house with smells of Christmas. ✓

> Ex: The gingerbread cookies were fresh out of the oven, filling the house with smells of Christmas. ✓

···

FRAGMENTS

Fragments are simply <u>incomplete sentences</u>. We can change the fragment into a complete sentence by making sure that it has a subject and a verb. The sentence should also make sense entirely on its own.

> Ex: The car that was parked outside. ✗

This sentence is incomplete. Although it contains a subject (the car) and a verb (was parked), it does not contain an *active* verb. The fact that the car was parked outside merely provides us **descriptive information** about the car, but there is no **action** in the sentence. It will not make sense unless we **add** or **delete** language.

> Ex: The car was parked outside. ✓

> Ex: The car that was parked outside was stolen. ✓

Verbs, often preceded by words like "who," "which," or "that," can simply be introducing descriptive information about the subject. <u>These alone cannot make a complete sentence</u>.

···

PARALLELISM

Parallelism is really a fancy way of saying "consistency." It is best to give the phrases or clauses within a sentence the same grammatical structure. This usually comes down to verb tense.

Ex: The student hated reading, writing, and to give oral presentations. ✗

The change in verb tense here is awkward and unnecessary. We can correct it by changing one or more of the phrases to match the others.

Ex: The student hated reading, writing, and giving oral presentations. ✓

Ex: The student hated to read, write, and give oral presentations. ✓

Either alternative is fine. The second option can be a bit more challenging when figuring out what to do with the preposition "to." We really only need one preposition, but if we see that it is being repeated earlier in the sentence, for the sake of consistency, we will repeat it for *all* the phrases.

Ex: The officer knew it was his duty **to** serve his community, **to** uphold the laws, and be a model citizen for others. ✗

Ex: The officer knew it was his duty **to** serve his community, **to** uphold the laws, and **to** be a model citizen for others. ✓

....

MISPLACED MODIFIERS

A **modifier** is a word or phrase that **describes** a noun or action in a sentence. Our job is to make sure that the modifying statement is **as close to the thing it is describing as possible.**

These statements very often open a sentence in the form of a dependent clause, so we need to **follow the comma immediately with the subject** pertaining to the modifier.

Ex: Walking home from school, the scenery and pleasant weather was the perfect way for Rebecca to decompress. ✗

This sentence, even though you can probably piece together what is being said, is technically not correct. That is precisely what makes these questions so difficult: it is not always easy to "hear" the mistake. **When the only difference in the answer choices is the order of the language, it is likely that this is the concept being tested.**

Ex: Walking home from school, Rebecca felt the scenery and pleasant weather was the perfect way to decompress. ✓

Think "who is walking home from school?" and immediately place the answer to that question after the comma.

You typically have control of the language found after the comma. If and when you have control of the language **BEFORE** the comma, choose a phrase that can **reasonably apply to whatever subject is found immediately after the comma.**

SUMMARY

- Go in order and answer the questions as you read.

- You may need to read on to answer certain questions (like picking a good introduction or transitional phrase).

- Do not focus solely on the underlined portions of the sentence.

- Make sure that the correction works for the <u>entire sentence</u> and that there are no bigger issues that need fixing.

- Be sure you identify *specifically* what is being underlined and what language the answer choices *actually* contain.

- If two answers seem "right," they're either both wrong or you've missed something.

- Eliminate answer choices that are essentially the same (like periods and semicolons).

- Simplify longer/difficult sentences (eliminate non-essential information, replace challenging words with simpler synonyms, etc.).

- Concise is nice — when in doubt, pick the shortest answer choice.

- Shorter answer choices should signal you to search for redundancies.

- Know your rules for punctuation. Don't rely solely on your ear (particularly for commas).

- When in doubt, pick the answer that's the least like the other three. This is especially helpful for subject-verb agreement questions.

- Properly identify the specific subject for questions dealing with verb tense or pronouns.

- Make sure that pronouns are sufficient.

- Avoid conversational/casual language.

- Study common word choice questions (affect vs. effect, then vs. than, its vs. it's).

- Know the difference between informal speech and written grammar.

- Make sure comparisons are logical and complete.

- When combining sentences, maintain the relationship between the original sentences. Avoid adding, removing, or rearranging language without cause.

- For word choice questions, focus on the specific situation to which the word in question applies. Do not select words just because they are familiar to you.

- For transition words, reread the sentence before and the sentence without the current transition word. Try to establish the relationship between those two sentences and pick an appropriate transition word. Study the commonly tested transition words.

- Pay close attention to physical questions (remember, not all the questions on this section come with actual questions). Circle the key words and figure out precisely what the question is asking for.

- For content-based questions, think about the "bigger picture." Add sentences that support the argument. Eliminate those that don't.

- Do not add sentences that are disruptive.

- Read answer justifications carefully and in their entirety. If you're unsure, use the justifications to guide your answers.

- Pick introductions/transitions that summarize the main ideas at that specific point in the passage.

- For passage conclusions, determine the main idea of the passage by rereading the title and briefly skimming through the passage (focus on the intro, conclusion, and first and last sentence of each paragraph).

- For sentence placement questions, try to find a link to another sentence in the paragraph (with a transition word, a direct reference, or some element of time). Do not be disruptive.

- Categorize the questions when you can. Determine what is at the root of the question. If you're struggling to categorize a question, it is likely an issue of sentence structure (parallelism, run ons, fragments, comma splices, misplaced modifiers).

SAT MATH

···

WHAT'S THE GIST?

The math section is broken down into two smaller parts: the **non-calculator section** and the **calculator section.**

The non-calculator section is the third section of the exam. You will have **25 minutes** to complete **20 questions.** 15 of those will be multiple choice questions with 4 possible answer choices. The remaining 5 will be grid-in questions. You will not be allowed a calculator.

The calculator math section is the fourth and final section of the exam. You will have **55 minutes** to complete **38 questions.** 30 of those will be multiple choice questions with 4 possible answer choices. The remaining 8 will be grid-in questions. You are allowed a calculator for the entirety of this section.

You will be provided with a brief reference sheet at the start of both the calculator and non-calculator sections.

WHAT CAN YOU EXPECT TO SEE?

Every exam is a bit different, but you can expect to see the following topics tested on each exam. Some of these topics are tested more frequently than others. Systems of linear equations, linear word problems, and quadratics, for example, are very commonly tested topics.

HEART OF ALGEBRA: (roughly 8 non-calculator questions, 11 calculator questions)

- Solving linear equations/inequalities
- Graphing linear equations
- Interpreting linear functions
- Linear inequality and equation word problems
- Solving systems of linear equations
- Systems of linear inequalities word problems

PASSPORT TO ADVANCED MATH: (roughly 9 non-calculator questions, 7 calculator questions)

- Solving quadratic equations
- Interpreting nonlinear expressions

- Quadratics and exponential word problems
- Radicals and rational exponents
- Operations with rational expressions and polynomials
- Polynomial factors and graphs
- Nonlinear equation graphs
- Linear and quadratic systems
- Isolating quantities
- Functions

PROBLEM SOLVING AND DATA ANALYTICS: (roughly 17 calculator questions)

- Ratios, rates, and proportions
- Percents
- Units
- Table data
- Scatterplots
- Key features of graphs
- Linear and exponential growth
- Data inferences
- Center, spread, and shape of distributions
- Data collection and conclusions

ADDITIONAL TOPICS IN MATH: (roughly 3 non-calculator questions, 3 calculator questions)

- Volume word problems
- Right triangle word problems
- Congruence and similarity
- Right triangle geometry
- Angles, arc lengths, and trigonometric functions
- Circle theorems
- Circle equations
- Complex numbers

STRATEGIES

Spend the time on the questions that are most likely to award you points. Each question is worth the same number of points, so you want to dedicate your time to the questions that are suited to your strengths first. The questions on this section get progressively harder, so you don't want to rush through the first half in an attempt to get to the final ones, when those questions might not go your way.

If math is not your strong suit and you're just looking to improve your score, then you shouldn't worry *too* much about those final questions. It's more important that you work diligently through the earlier questions so that you are not misreading or making careless mistakes.

That being said, the level of difficulty will reset once you reach the grid-in questions on both the calculator and non-calculator sections. Use that to your advantage. **When you feel as though you have a hit a wall with the multiple choice questions, consider skipping ahead to the grid-ins.** The first few are usually pretty straightforward and manageable. Tackling those easier grid-in questions will ensure that you are making the best use of your time and will provide you with a boost of confidence (which can help when you revisit the multiple choice questions).

You don't need to master all of the difficult topics to do well on this section, but you *should* **solidify your basics.** Many students won't review the simpler topics, but this is a mistake. You need to refresh your memory on the concepts that you may have learned before you even got to high school. **This includes performing basic operations (adding, subtracting, multiplying, dividing) by hand**, a necessary skill for the non-calculator math section. We will discuss some of these operations later.

You also want to be sure that you **solidify the most commonly tested concepts**. The content and format of the SAT math section tend to be rather predictable, so the more you practice, the more familiar you will become with these concepts. Be sure that you address any issues with those core topics at the onset of (and throughout) your studying. We will discuss several of those topics — systems of equations, linear word problems, manipulating algebraic expressions, etc. — in greater detail later.

....

Let's talk about how to avoid some common mistakes on the actual exam.

When permitted, use your calculator wisely. The calculator is a blessing and a curse: if you're not careful it can lead you in the wrong direction. You don't want to trust it unquestioningly; you should always be mentally checking to see if what it's spitting out makes sense. This is especially important with negative numbers and exponents. Here are some calculator tips to avoid these mishaps:

- Input things one step at a time and avoid one long string of text
- Use parentheses when dealing with negatives and exponents
- Double check to make sure you are in the correct mode, especially when dealing with angles (usually degree, not radian)

While we're on the topic of calculators, remember that you can OBSERVE a lot of things with the graphing function. Any questions dealing with the behavior of a function or graph — minimums/ maximums, intercepts, zeros, points of intersections with other graphs, asymptotes, points of discontinuity — can be answered by graphing and observing.

You can use the graphing component of your calculator to solve annoying equations. If you have a really ugly equation you don't want to solve by hand, put one side of the equation into one y= and the other side of the equation into another y=, graph them, and find where the two graphs intersect.

Back to our strategies. **Make sure you double check what the question is asking for.** You can even circle the question itself if you need to. Very often, you may solve an equation properly, but lose points because you ignore what they're actually looking for. This is especially problematic for equations with more than one variable, and geometry problems where you might have a lot of elements going on at once. If the question asks for the width, make sure you give the width and not the length, or vice versa. **Get in the habit of rereading the last line of the question AFTER you've completed your calculations.** It's easy to forget what you were solving for, so give yourself a reminder. Don't default to solving an equation, circling that choice, and moving on.

Also be sure to **keep track of your variables** and know what they represent. You don't always have to use "x" and "y." If a word problem has to do with bracelets and necklaces, use "b" to represent bracelets and "n" to represent necklaces. It's easier to keep track of what your variables mean this way.

Circle key words/phrases in the question. This will help you break up some of the wordier problems by visually indicating what's important, but it will also keep you from ignoring some of the specific requirements they laid out for you. Terms like odd/even, positive/negative, rational/irrational, smallest/ largest, prime, integeter, two-digit are all crucial characteristics that will change the scope of the problem.

Look out for any capitalized or italicized language, especially when units of measurement are involved. The italics are probably indicating there's a mixture of units. <u>If they give you a unit conversion at the end of the problem, that's also a pretty big sign that you need to be mindful of the units in the problem and do some converting.</u>

Keep an eye out for one of the biggest pitfalls of all: mishandling negatives. Careless mistakes are bound to happen, but if you deal with signed numbers carefully, you'll avoid selecting trap answer choices. The SAT will always predict the most common careless errors students will make and provide answer choices that line up with those missteps, so you have to be detail-oriented even on the simplest of problems. Many of these errors involve mishandling negative signs and can appear correct if not double-checked. **Pay attention to the order of operations, too.** If careless mistakes are an ongoing issue, be sure to check your answers after solving. Plug your answer back into the original equation if there is one, and see if it works out. It may seem like a time waster, but ultimately, you'll only be using up a few seconds and you can catch mistakes easily this way.

Let's talk about what to do if you don't know how to get started with a problem. That's a common issue, because you might be familiar with the relevant topics and formulas, but the material could be presented in a way that you've never seen before. When you don't have a procedure in mind, you have to ask yourself some prompting questions to get the ball rolling. That will get easier the more you practice.

Start by writing down a formula when you can (see formula sheet). If you can figure out which concept is being tested, write out the formulas you know regarding that topic. The average/mean formula, for example, is a commonly tested one. After you've written down the formula, revisit the text and determine what they've given you directly (or indirectly) and plug those values into the formula. You may need to revisit the formula more than once or use multiple formulas, but your job will mostly be figuring out what's been given, what can be determined with a little work, and ultimately the value you need to calculate.

You don't really think to write out certain formulas. You may default to doing an operation right away, but you can easily make mistakes this way. You might divide instead of multiplying when you're trying to do something theoretically vs. actually writing out the steps. Theoretical operations also won't help for trickier problems where there are variables involved and not everything is given to you strictly numerically. So don't underestimate the power of physically writing out the formula.

Step "outside" the problem. When things start to feel overwhelming, don't focus on the specifics of the problem. Start by identifying the underlying concept being tested. Once you have the concept, think of a formula or procedure that aligns with that concept. Then step back "in" the problem and determine what you've been given and what you still need. This type of simplification is especially important for grouped questions. These grouped questions, where multiple questions focus on one scenario or graph, can be visually overstimulating if you allow yourself to get distracted by all the presented information (a good portion of which may not be relevant or necessary for individual questions).

When in doubt, just start manipulating an expression or equation any way that you can. When you don't know exactly how to solve a problem, try to play around with the equation, even if you're not exactly sure *why*. Think less about what you "*should*" do and more about what you "*could*" do. Ask yourself if you can: distribute, factor, combine like terms or group similar terms to one side of an equation, or expand. Those are the core four methods of manipulation, as they will apply to any number of expressions/equations. Every time you perform an action, run through the list again until you get to an end result. Other manipulation techniques (like cross multiplying, polynomial long division, or multiplying by a conjugate) will apply only to <u>specific</u> types of equations/expressions. More on that later!

Speaking of manipulating, **you may need to tweak your answer** after you solve something correctly. If you're fairly confident you've worked through something correctly, but then look at the answer choices and don't see yours listed, don't panic. If it's algebraic, they may have reworked the expression into a similar form. If it's numerical, you may have calculated your answer in a different form. You may end up with a decimal only to see answers written as fractions, or radicals, or in terms of pi. You'll simply just need to figure out which of the answer choices matches up to yours by putting the answer choices into the calculator to determine their values.

Keep in mind that answer choices that are *close* to the one you got but not quite the same are probably wrong. "x-y" looks a whole lot like "y-x" but they are very different things. If they ask for a value "closest to" the answer or ask for an approximation, that's when you can pick an answer choice that's close numerically. But if that is not specified, or if the choices are algebraic, answers that are similar but still different are likely incorrect.

Try to eliminate answer choices, even when you don't know how to fully solve a problem. Process of elimination is something students default to for the other sections, but won't utilize on the math section. It's not as habitual; you may see a problem, think "I don't know how to do that" and move on. But you should always try to eliminate as many choices as possible to give yourself better odds when guessing. You may not know enough to solve entirely, but you might know enough about a topic to eliminate even one or two choices. Try to force yourself not to give up. Focus on what you DO know about a topic and see if that gives you enough information to narrow it down.

Remember that the SAT provides you with a small reference sheet (pictured below). Formulas for area and volume can be found here. You may find this reference sheet particularly helpful if you have a tendency to mix up related formulas, like those for the <u>area and circumference of a circle</u>. Use the formula sheet to your advantage!

The special triangles and the information regarding the number of degrees/radian in a circle is especially useful. The special triangles do not pop up on the exam *too* often, but the questions involving them can usually be solved if you refer to the formulas and remain detail-oriented. If a problem contains $\sqrt{2}$, $\sqrt{3}$, or angle measures of 30/60/45, you should make sure to circle back to the reference sheet.

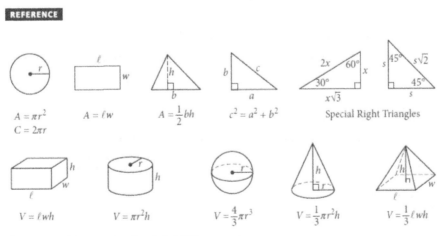

The number of degrees of arc in a circle is 360.
The number of radians of arc in a circle is 2π.
The sum of the measures in degrees of the angles of a triangle is 180.

Let's wrap up with a few general tips. **Mark up diagrams or draw your own.** Visualizations (especially with geometry problems) can make all the difference, so draw out the scenario or figure if it's not provided for you. If you're given something in the x-y plane, draw out the plane and physically plot the points. If it's a word problem that you can break down and visually represent somehow, do that. Graphics will be easier to absorb than a giant chunk of text.

Don't be afraid to play around with the figures they provide. They always give you enough information to solve a problem, but sometimes you have to get creative and fill in some of the visual gaps. For circle problems, sometimes rotating the radius or drawing a new one is helpful. Drawing lines to create new triangles is also a great tool. Even rotating the figures or taking a figure made up of several shapes and redrawing the shapes individually can help a great deal.

Get comfortable translating word problems into equations. Modeling equations from words is an important skill. Know that "more/larger than" signifies addition, "less/fewer than" indicates subtraction, "times as great" indicates multiplication, and the word "is" represents an equal sign. We will discuss this in greater detail later.

Look for patterns and identities, especially on the non-calculator section. Most of the time you can work your way around having to know the identities, but for the purpose of saving time, they can be really helpful. Special triangles, like the 3-4-5 or 5-12-13 triangles, can shave valuable seconds off a problem if you recognize the pattern and don't default to Pythagorean Theorem. This is crucial for the non-calculator math section. <u>If you feel as though it is unreasonable to perform the necessary calculations to solve a problem by hand, an identity is likely built into the problem.</u>

Lastly, **remember that there is often more than one way to solve a problem**. You don't have to solve it the way the SAT wants you to. You can solve things logically, algebraically, or graphically. Check out the calculator tips and tricks to find ways of testing for equivalency or solving difficult equations with the graphing component of your calculator. **You can also backsolve or use test values if you're truly stuck.** On that note, be careful using 0, 1 or 2 as test values. And if you do decide to plug in the answer choices, start with the middlemost value. You may be able to determine if you need a larger number or smaller number based on what you observe.

Above all, manage your time well. There's not much time to be stubborn, particularly on the non-calculator section, so if a problem is not going your way, skip it and come back to it. The importance of revisiting a problem with fresh eyes can't be stressed enough. Staring at something for too long won't help, but very often when you come back to it later on, something will click. And you won't be chewing up the clock this way. Leave yourself enough time to revisit those questions at the end of the section. Do not waste time on questions that you know how to solve but that will take a substantial amount of time. Some questions are simply time-sucking questions. You need to be wise enough to leave those until last and only attempt them if you have confidently tackled all the other problems. Remember our 5- second rule!

FUNDAMENTAL REVIEW

As far as subject matter goes, there is no better way to prepare than to work through several SATs. As we stated before, each exam is a little different, so it will take working through a substantial amount of tests before you feel like you've been exposed to all of the possible content.

It's not enough to simply familiarize yourself with the relevant formulas/concepts; you need to think about HOW the information is being presented to you on the exam. There is no better way to master this than to work through several exams. You'll start to recognize patterns in the way the questions are worded. Make note of these patterns. **Determine what key phrases or elements of a question clue you in on what's being tested.** Test yourself on that knowledge just as much as you would a formula. Your notes, flashcards, or review sheets should contain bits of information like this. Here's an example:

> Q: "When a question gives me 3 values and asks for a fourth...."
>
> A: "I'll probably need to set up a proportion"

Before you start to tackle all of the possible topics and questions, **you must first make sure that you have mastered your basics.** After all, you have to walk before you can run!

Fundamentals are crucial for two reasons. For starters, the earlier questions on both math sections will focus more heavily on these foundational skills. But the later, more complex questions will also require knowledge of these concepts. Math is a subject that inherently builds on itself, so it's nearly impossible to master the challenging material without giving yourself a solid foundation.

The following sections will recap some of these basic skills by:

- Reviewing definitions and properties of numbers
- Reviewing basic operations/concepts: plugging in (and function notation), isolating/solving for a variable, modeling equations, factoring, probability, proportions, angle properties, percents, properties of lines, rules for exponents, exponential growth, etc.
- Listing some basic formulas

....

DEFINITIONS AND PROPERTIES OF NUMBERS

Integers are positive and negative whole numbers (so no fractions or decimals). Zero is also considered an integer.

Rational numbers are all numbers that can be written as a fraction of integers. This includes fractions (obviously), whole numbers, finite decimals, and repeating decimals. A decimal like .3333333, for example, is the same thing as ⅓ — so it is considered rational. Essentially, rational numbers are the "pretty" numbers; they work out neatly.

Irrational numbers are numbers that can't be put into fraction form. They are very often radicals. The square root of 2, for example, is irrational. If you put it into your calculator, you will get a long, non-repeating decimal. Basically, irrational numbers are the "ugly" numbers; they *don't* work out neatly.

Prime numbers are numbers that are only divisible by themselves and 1. Examples of primes are 2, 3, 5, 7, 11, 13, etc. Keep in mind that 2 is the only even prime number.

Multiples of a number are all numbers divisible by that number. 16 is a multiple of 4 because 16/4 = 4 and not some decimal.

Factors of a number are all the numbers that divide evenly into that number. 5 is a factor of 40 because 40/5 = 8.

....

Properties/Behavior of Basic Operations

Even + Even = Even	2 + 2 = 4
Odd + Odd = Even	3 + 3 = 6
Odd + Even = Odd	3 + 2 = 5
Even x Even = Even	2 x 2 = 4
Odd x Odd = Odd	3 x 3 = 9
Even x Odd = Even	2 x 3 = 6
Positive x Positive = Positive	2 x 2 = 4
Negative x Negative = Positive	(-2) x (-2) = 4
Negative x Positive = Negative	(-2) x 2 = -4
Positive/ Negative = Negative	4 / (-2) = -2

A negative number raised to an EVEN exponent will give a POSITIVE result.

$$(-2)^2 = 4$$

A negative number raised to an ODD exponent will give a NEGATIVE result.

$$(-2)^3 = -8$$

When you subtract a negative number, that is the same thing as ADDING that number.

$$5 - (-3) = 5 + 3 = 8$$

....

SIMPLE SOLVING/ ISOLATING A VARIABLE

Solving for a single variable is an important skill, so if it is something you struggle with, make sure to practice this a lot. Not only will you have purely algebraic problems that require you to solve in this way, it's also the last step for a lot of the word problems or modeling problems you'll encounter.

Remember that when you're getting a variable alone, you're essentially "undoing" anything that's been done to it by performing the "opposite" operation.

- **Addition** is the opposite of **subtraction**
- **Multiplication** is the opposite of **division**
- Taking a **square root** is the opposite of **squaring**

You'll want to "undo" these operations one step at a time in the **opposite** order of PEMDAS. (Although, there are always exceptions to this rule – more on that later!)

So if we have something like:

$$\frac{2}{3}x^2 + 6 = 12$$

We'd start by undoing the addition of 6 by subtracting 6 from each side.

$$\frac{2}{3}x^2 = 6$$

Then we would undo the multiplication of ⅔ by dividing by ⅔. **This is the same thing as multiplying by the reciprocal**– in this case, $\frac{3}{2}$

$$\left(\frac{3}{2}\right)\frac{2}{3}x^2 = 6\left(\frac{3}{2}\right) \Rightarrow x^2 = 9$$

Then we would undo the square by taking the square root of both sides. **When solving for a variable, don't forget to consider both the positive and negative square roots.**

$$\sqrt{x^2} = \sqrt{9} \Rightarrow x = \pm 3$$

You can't assume that every addition/subtraction can be eliminated first. Things get a bit trickier when the expressions get more involved. But the idea is simple enough: deal with the "bigger" problems first. It's sort of like peeling an onion.: if something is being done to the *entire* expression, that's the first thing to tackle. The first step does NOT always involve addition/subtraction.

Here's an example:

$$\frac{2x^2 + 6}{3} = 12$$

This equation looks almost identical to the first one we went over, but it is a very different problem. We can't just subtract the 6 from the start. The division by 3 is the "bigger" problem. It's not just the x term being divided by 3 – it's the *entire* left side of the equation, so we have to address this first.

We would start by multiplying both sides of the equation by 3.

$$2x^2 + 6 = 36$$

Now that we've dealt with the only "bigger" issue, we're free to solve for x normally. Use the following process:

1) Subtract the 6
2) Divide by 2
3) Take the square root

One more example:

$$\sqrt{2x + 10} = (4)$$

We would begin by squaring both sides (as the square root is the "biggest" problem):

$$(\sqrt{2x + 10})^2 = (4)^2$$

$$2x + 10 = 16$$

Then, we subtract 10 from both sides:

2x = 6

And finally divide each side by 2:

x = 3

Note: Inequalities containing variables will be dealt with the same way a standard equation is dealt with. **The only major difference is that multiplying or dividing by a negative will change the direction of the inequality.** Otherwise, the process for isolating the variable is the same!

....

Isolating a variable will not always result in a numerical answer. Sometimes you'll just end up shifting things in the original equation around so that the variable you care about is alone on one side of the equation. You won't necessarily be working strictly with numbers, but the **same rules apply**. You'll want to undo any operations being performed on that variable.

Conceptually, it probably makes more sense to subtract 3 from something than it does to subtract "y" from something. But that "y" is just a placeholder for a number, so you can work with variables just as you work with numbers. Recall that **you can only combine like terms**. For example:

- Numbers can be combined with other numbers
- x terms can be combined with other x terms
- x^2 terms can be combined with other x^2 terms

You can only combine variables of the **same name and degree** (have the same exponent). Anything else just doesn't make sense!

- x terms **CANNOT** be combine with x^2 terms
- Variables **CANNOT** be combined with numbers

Let's work through an example:

$$\frac{g^2 + B}{4} = M$$

Suppose the question asked us to "solve for *g*" or to "get *g* in terms of D and M." Both of these phrases mean the same thing: to get *g* alone on one side of the equation.

We will work through this the same way we did our earlier examples. We will deal with the 4 first by multiplying both sides of the equation by 4.

$$g^2 + B = 4M$$

Now we can't really multiply the 4 by M to get an actual value; we can only leave it as 4 x M (or 4M). Next, we would deal with the B by subtracting it from both sides of the equation.

$$g^2 = 4M - B$$

We can't actually subtract B from 4M. We can only write it as "4M-B." Our last step is then to take the square root of both sides.

$$g = \pm\sqrt{4M - B}$$

It's not quite as satisfying as ending up with a tangible number, but your job is done!

....

PLUGGING IN

Plugging in values is a simple concept, but that doesn't mean you should rush through it. (After all, sometimes the easiest things are the easiest to mess up). Several problems on the exam will ask that you simply plug certain values into an expression. But that's not the only way we can use plugging in to our benefit. **It's also a great way to "check" our answers** after we've solved for a variable. Remember, this is especially important if you find that you make a lot of careless mistakes with your calculations. Checking your answer choices by plugging them back in can help you identify an error in your calculations.

Plugging in can also **provide us with a back-up plan when we don't know how to solve something algebraically.** You might remember from our strategies that there is often more than one way to solve a problem. **Backsolving (sometimes referred to as PITA: plug in the answers) is an effective strategy to utilize when you don't know how to solve a problem algebraically or think the algebraic approach is too long/complicated.**

As far as the actual process goes, plugging in essentially just means that you're **replacing a variable with an actual value** (usually a number —in more complex cases, another variable/expression). When you're only dealing with numbers, this can be done pretty easily with your calculator. Just be sure that you input the values carefully and make good use of parentheses (especially when negatives and exponents are involved).

....

The concept of plugging in goes hand in hand with **function notation**. You've probably seen f(x), g(x), or some variation of this before. F(x) is usually read as "f of x," which means we have some function, f, whose values are determined by inputting different values for x. It doesn't matter if it's a number, another variable, or even an entire expression. The procedure is the same: **replace x with whatever appears inside the parentheses**. Don't get spooked by questions involving function notation just because they look tricky. It usually ends up being pretty basic algebra.

f(3) would simply be whatever value we get after plugging in 3. Remember, "plugging in" just means replacing, so replace x with 3 anywhere it appears in the function.

Here's an example:

$$f(x) = \frac{x^2 - 3x}{4}$$

What is $f(-3)$?

By simply replacing x with -3 in the expression, we'll end up with our answer. Remember to use parentheses carefully if inputting in the calculator.

$$f(-3) = \frac{(-3)^2 - 3(-3)}{4} \implies \frac{18}{4}$$

When there are two functions defined, sometimes you will be asked to calculate a composite function, which is when one function gets substituted into the other. There are two major notations for this:

1) $f(g(x))$
2) $f \circ g(x)$

Both are read as "f of g of x." You will probably see the first notation more often. The important thing to remember is to **start with the "inner" function** or the function that appears **closer to the variable**. The same idea applies: you will replace the variables with whatever value or expression appears in the parentheses. Let's work through an example:

$$f(x) = 5x - 1 \qquad g(x) = x^2 + 3$$

To calculate $f(g(x))$, we would replace x with g(x) wherever x appears in f.

$$f(g(x)) = 5(x^2 + 3) - 1$$

We can then clean things up by distributing and combining like terms. Let's take it one step further and input a value for x.

$$f(g(5)) = 5((5)^2 + 3) - 1$$

Note: $fg(x)$ is NOT the same as a composite function. If the "∘" symbol is missing, this means the functions are being multiplied by each other, not composed.

FACTORING

Factoring is a helpful tool for rewriting expressions or determining the zeros of a polynomial. Zeros, roots, solutions, and x-intercepts all mean the same thing: whatever x values will make the function equal to 0. There are three basic types of factoring we will review:

1) Factoring a trinomial (usually a quadratic)

2) Pulling out a GCF

3) Difference of two squares

TRINOMIALS

A trinomial is a polynomial with three terms, very often quadratics with a front term (usually x) that is squared.

The standard form of a quadratic is:

$$ax^2 + bx + c$$

To factor a quadratic whose leading coefficient (a) is equal to 1, you must find two integers that multiply to c and add to b. It's a way of anticipating what would happen if you used FOIL to go back from the factored form of the quadratic to the original equation.

Ex: $x^2 + 5x + 4$

Two numbers that multiply to 4 and add to 5 are 4 and 1, so in factored form, this trinomial will look like:

$$(x + 4)(x + 1)$$

To calculate the zeros (sometimes called solutions) of a polynomial, bring all terms to one side of an equation and factor. Then **take each factor, set it equal to 0, and solve for x**. If either of the expressions in the parentheses can be made to equal zero, then the whole expression will equal zero, because anything times zero is zero.

$$(x + 4)(x + 1) = 0$$

$$
\begin{array}{ll}
x + 4 = 0 & x + 1 = 0 \\
\underline{-4 \quad -4} & \underline{-1 \quad -1} \\
x = -4 & x = -1
\end{array}
$$

If all of the terms are not on one side of an equation, you must first move everything to one side and combine like terms before factoring.

$$
\begin{array}{l}
x^2 + x - 8 = 3x - 7 \\
\underline{-3x + 7 \quad -3x + 7} \\
x^2 - 2x - 1 = 0
\end{array}
$$

If you cannot find two integers that will multiply to c and add to b, you must use the quadratic formula to find the roots:

$$\frac{-b \pm \sqrt{b^2 - 4ac}}{2a}$$

The quadratic formula will work for any quadratic, not just the ones that won't factor easily by hand. Quadratics with leading coefficients not equal to 1 are good examples of quadratics best solved with the quadratic formula.

FACTORING WITH A GCF

Sometimes the only way to factor is with a greatest common factor (GCF). The GCF is a number/term that all of your original terms are multiples of. You will "pull out" that term in front and leave what is "left over" from each original term in a set of parentheses. When you "pull out" a term, you are essentially dividing.

To determine the GCF, look first for a number that divides into all of the terms' coefficients. Then see if there are any variables in common. You can pull out the term with the *lowest* degree (exponent).

Here's an example:

$$4x^5 - 16x^2$$

The two terms both have a numerical factor of 4. They also share an x variable. The lowest degree of either term is 2, so we can pull out an x2.

$$4x^2\left(x^3 - 4\right)$$

GCF

What's left over when we divided the first term by the GCF

What's left over when we divided the second term by the GCF

Note: You can reform the original expression by distributing the 4x².

Note: When we divide terms with exponents, we **subtract** exponents

Note: If a term is completely divisible by the GCF, **it does not disappear**. We need to put a "1" in its place.

DIFFERENCE OF TWO SQUARES

A difference of two squares, as the name suggests, is a two-term polynomial where one term is being subtracted from the other. These are typically both perfect square terms (meaning they have whole number square roots).

To factor:

1) Draw two sets of parentheses.

2) Place the square root of the first term at the front of each set of parentheses.

3) Place the square root of the second term at the back of each set of parentheses.

4) Put an addition sign in one set of parentheses and a subtraction sign in the other.

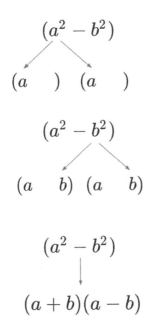

No matter what the method of factoring, to determine a polynomial's roots/zeros, simply take each factor, set it equal to zero, and solve for x. **All polynomials are divisible by** $(x - k)$ **if** k **is a root.**

MODELING

Let's move on now to modeling. Modeling is essentially a process of building equations or expressions from a word problem. Sometimes you will then have to solve for the variable (or variables), but sometimes you'll just be asked to model the equation!

Get familiar with the most common language.

- **"Is"** translates to an equal sign.
- **"More than, larger than, longer than,"** and **"sum"** translate to addition.
- **"Less than, smaller than, shorter than,"** and **"difference"** translate to subtraction
- **"Times as much"** and **"product"** translate to multiplication

Also look for words like "per," "each," and "every." These typically mean that multiplication by a variable is necessary. If there's some numerical <u>value</u> (whether it be cost, price, weight, volume) associated with a variable, you will **multiply** that value by the variable to determine a <u>total</u> cost/price/weight/volume.

For example, if a worker earns 15 dollars *per* hour, the **total earnings** would be found by taking that individual value (15) and multiplying by the number of hours. If the number of hours is unknown, we use a variable in its place. You will see later in this chapter that the total cost formula is one of the most commonly tested formulas on the SAT. It goes hand in hand with modeling problems.

It's important to be detail-oriented with modeling problems. Avoid careless mistakes by **modeling the equation(s) *as you read through the text***. Try not to read through the entire problem and then search for the specific variables and figures afterwards. It's very likely that your eye will accidentally pair the wrong value with the wrong variable if you take that approach. Instead, read the sentences one at a time and write your equations as you read through the text.

....

PROBABILITY

Probability is the likelihood that an event will occur. Questions involving probability are typically very straightforward, but you need to be detail-oriented. The key idea is that probability is written as a fraction where the number of **total possible outcomes** is your denominator and the number of **desired outcomes** is your numerator.

$$Probability = \frac{desired\ outcomes}{total\ outcomes}$$

So, if a bowl contains 20 marbles and 8 of them are red, the probability of selecting a red marble is:

$$\frac{\#\ of\ red\ marbles}{\#\ of\ total\ marbles} = \frac{8}{20}$$

Slightly fancier problems will deal with *conditional* probability. We will discuss that topic later on.

PROPORTIONS

Proportions are used to determine a missing value in a relationship. **When we are given one complete relationship between two variables and one *incomplete* relationship between two variables of the same kind, we will set up a portion.** Note that proportions are always related to one another through some sort of **scale factor**, which is basically fancy language for multiplication. One relationship is always being multiplied or divided by something to give us the second relationship.

Proportions can pop up in a number of scenarios. They can be part of a word problem (recipes and surveys are common) or part of a geometry problem (like questions involving similar triangles or scale drawings). They can be used to convert units, and they can even appear in trigonometry. The important thing is identifying when to use them, and s**etting them up carefully.** There's always more than one way to set up a proportion, but you should always keep things **consistent and properly arranged**. This is a concept more easily understood through example.

If a recipe calls for 2 eggs and 5 cups of flour, but you want to alter the recipe to use 3 eggs, how many cups of flour would you need?

Let's start with the relationship we know. We know for certain that 2 eggs will be paired with 5 cups of flour. We'll use that to set up the left side of the equation.

$$\frac{2}{5} = \frac{?}{?}$$

To properly set up the right side, we need to make sure we maintain the pattern on the left side. We placed the number of eggs on top, and the cups of flour on the bottom, so we will do the same on the right side. We already know that 3 eggs will be used, so we will place the 3 in the **numerator** of the right fraction. Since we don't know how many cups of flours we need, we will put an x in the **denominator**.

$$\frac{2 \; eggs}{5 \; cups} = \frac{3 \; eggs}{x \; cups}$$

Once the proportion is properly set up, all you have to do is cross multiply and solve for x. *If you had set up the first fraction upside-down, with the number of cups on top of the number of eggs, you'd arrive at the same answer as long as the other fraction was arranged the same way.*

PERCENTS

Percents are used **to indicate portions of a whole.** You will see them frequently in word problems dealing with tax or discounts. Regardless of the specifics of the problem, the first thing you want to do is **change the percent into decimal form** so that it can be used to perform actual calculations.

To do that, we simply take the decimal and move it two spaces **to the left**. You have to be careful and make sure you move it the *full* two spaces and use a zero as a place holder if necessary. For example, 5% is **not** .5. It is .05.

Sometimes it's difficult to figure out which value in a problem should be multiplied by the actual percentage. **Look for the word "of" to help you.** Whatever you're taking the percentage **"OF"** is what should be multiplied by the percent. Sometimes that will be an unknown value, so we'll multiply the percentage by a variable. If a question reads "30 is 10% of what number," you can't just multiply .10 by 30. You want 10% **OF** some unknown value, so the percent (.10) will be multiplied by a variable. The equation would read: .1x = 30

If the percent is part of a bigger word problem, more work may be involved. The procedure after you've calculated the percentage will come down to the specifics of the problem and you'll have to use your judgement to arrange the equation correctly. If it's a problem involving tax, you're going to be <u>adding</u> that value to your initial cost. Interest on loans or savings accounts typically indicate growth, so you will <u>add</u> values in these circumstances as well. If it's a discount, you'll be <u>subtracting</u> that value from the initial amount. Decay or any sort of decline will also indicate <u>subtraction</u>.

Word problems like this can very often be dealt with in ONE step by using a simplified version of the exponential growth formula.

$$A = I(1 \pm r)^t$$

In this formula, I represents the initial value, r represents the rate (or percentage) written as a decimal, t represents time, and A represents the final value of the growth. Because problems dealing with tax or sales are only happening once, we can replace t with "1" and ignore it after that.

If an item has an original price of $60 dollars and you receive a discount of 25%, you can use this formula to calculate the final amount (A) in one step. The initial price (I) is 60. The rate (r) is .25. Since it is a discount, we will SUBTRACT the .25 from 1.

$$A = 60 (1 - .25)$$
$$A = 60 (.75)$$
$$A = 45$$

EXPONENTIAL GROWTH

The SAT mostly focuses on the version of the exponential growth formula that we just discussed, but you may sometimes have to use a more complex version of that formula:

$$A = I(1 \pm \tfrac{r}{n})^{nt}$$

Here, *I* still represents the initial value, *r* represents the rate (or percentage) written as a decimal, *t* represents time, and *A* represents the final value of growth. *T* is typically measured in years, but interest is not alwasy calculated on *yearly* basis. So what do we do? That's what *n* helps to answer. **n represents the number of times interest is compounded in 1 year.** This is best shown by example:

> Suppose a bank guarantees that an investment of $100 will grow with a montly interest rate of 5%, compounded *monthly*. How much money will accrue after 5 years?

The varying units of time (*t*) might confuse you. The interest is compounded montly, but you're asked to calculate a total in years. Since t = 5 years, you'll need to use *n* to represent that the interest is compounded *monthly*, or 12 times per 1 year.

So the correct equation is:

$$A = 100(1 + .05)^{12 \times 5}$$
$$A = 100(1 + .05)^{60}$$

If the interest rate had been given as a *yearly* interest rate, you would have needed to adjust the interest rate in the formula to turn it into a *monthly* rate. Luckily, you were given the monthly rate, so we didn't need to convert the rate. Other questions may require that conversion. Let's look at an example:

> Julia invests 500 dollars into a bank account with a yearly interest rate of 6%. compounded weekly. How much money will she have after 3 years?

Since t= 5 years and the interest compounds *weekly*, you'll need to multiply the total years by the *number of times the interest compounds per year*, in this case 52. You'll also need to adjust the interest rate. Since the interest rate was *yearly*, but it is compounded *weekly*, you'll need to divide .06 by the number of times the interest combounds per year, again 52, to determine the *weekly* rate:

$$A = 500\left(1 + \frac{.06}{52}\right)^{52 \times 5}$$
$$A = 500(1 + .001153)^{260}$$

When you're dealing with interest rates that are compounded *fewer than one time* within the scope of the problem, like when you have interest that's compounded *every two years* but you want to know how much money will accrue after *one year*, **n may need to be a fraction.**

....

ANGLE PROPERTIES

Properties of angles are simple enough if you can commit them to memory. The 4 that are the most important are:

1) Angles that lie on a straight line will add up to 180 degrees.

2) Angles in a triangle will add up to 180 degrees.

3) Vertical angles (opposite angles formed by two intersecting lines) are congruent.

4) Alternate interior angles are congruent.

$a + b = 180°$

It's also helpful to know that **angles opposite congruent sides in a triangle are also congruent.**

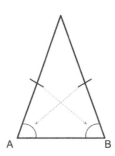

Questions with figures containing missing angles will usually require you to use some combination of these rules. Just fill in the figure one angle measure at a time with these guidelines until you arrive at the angle in question.

....

PROPERTIES OF LINES

Lines are used to represent **steady** change from a fixed starting point. For each bit you run, you rise the same amount. While the equation of a line can be presented to you in many ways, a very useful lens through which to view it is the standard form below

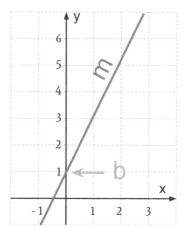

Equation of a Line

$$y = mx + b$$

Slope (m) is how quickly the line is changing. A large value of "m" makes a line steep; a small value makes it shallow. The formula for slope has a few different variations, the most common being:

$$m = \frac{y_1 - y_2}{x_1 - x_2}$$

This version is most helpful when given two points. Whichever point you choose for "y_2" doesn't matter, as long as you make sure to include the corresponding coordinate as "x_2."

Slope is also very often referred to as:

$$\frac{rise}{run} \quad \text{or} \quad \frac{change\ in\ y}{change\ in\ x}$$

Note: Not all linear equations will use the variables "x" and "y"; those are simply the variables we are most familiar with. If you are given an equation with different variables, determine which variable is acting as your "y" and which one is acting as your "x." The "y," which is your **dependent variable**, is typically alone on one side of the equation.

....

The y intercept is the point on the y-axis where the line crosses over. This is the "b" term in our standard equation.

When asked about the slope or y-intercept of a line, it is crucial that you **first isolate y**. Once you have the equation in standard form, those values are **clearly presented** as constants in the equation.

....

Lastly, you should know how parallel lines and perpendicular lines relate to one another algebraically.

- The slopes of **parallel** lines are **equal**
- The slope of **perpendicular** lines are **negative reciprocals** of one another

BASIC FORMULAS

$$Average = \frac{Sum}{Number\ of\ Terms}$$

....

Total cost (Weight/Price/volume) = Individual cost × number of units

....

$$Velocity = \frac{Distance}{time}$$

Note: Be sure units are consistent. If speed is given in miles per hour, the distance must be in miles and the time in hours.

....

The **Pythagorean Theorem** relates the lengths of the sides of a right triangle. For the triangle below, it would be:

$$a^2 + b^2 = c^2$$

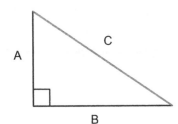

It is important to note here that the "c" term in this formula is the hypotenuse, the longest side, of the triangle. While the "a" and "b" terms are interchangeable, the "c" term is not. When you plug in, be sure to put the longest side there.

....

To find the **Distance** between two points, $P_1 = (X_1, Y_1)$ and $P_2 = (X_2, Y_2)$, you just find the difference of the X and Y values for each point and plug those into the Pythagorean Theorem:

$$Distance = d = \sqrt{(x_1 - x_2)^2 + (y_1 - y_2)^2}$$

....

$$\text{Percent Increase/Decrease} = \frac{Final - Initial}{Initial} \times 100$$

....

RULES FOR EXPONENTS

You will see a more detailed collection of rules for exponents on the formula sheet, but the following are the most commonly tested and the most crucial to remember.

$$a^x a^y = a^{x+y} \qquad\qquad \frac{a^x}{a^y} = a^{x-y}$$

$$\left(a^x\right)^y = a^{xy} \qquad\qquad a^{\frac{x}{y}} = \sqrt[y]{a^x}$$

There are several topics that appear regularly on the SAT. You will find these topics on both the calculator and non-calculator sections presented as both multiple choice and grid-in questions. **You will want to make sure to nail down these topics because they're tested so frequently.** Coupled with the foundational skills discussed earlier, a strong grasp of these concepts will ensure that you can tackle a substantial number of problems.

....

LINEAR WORD PROBLEMS

The topic of lines as a whole is extremely important for the SAT math sections. We already addressed the equation of a line and some important properties of lines earlier, but the goal now is to understand how those properties apply to word problems.

The two most important elements of a line are the **slope** and the **y-intercept**. When dealing with a word problem, terminology like "slope" and "y-intercept" don't make sense, since we are no longer dealing with a physical graph. We must broaden our understanding of these terms and recognize what terminology does make sense in the context of a real world problem.

....

Let's start with the slope: the slope represents the *rate of change*. More specifically, it tells us how much our dependent variable changes in relation to our independent variable. Since the **slope** relates to the rate of change, when asked what the slope of a linear equation represents, we will use words like **"increase/decrease," "per," "each," "every," and "additional."**

The y-intercept represents an initial value. It is a value that is unaffected by the independent variable (like a fixed cost or one-time fee). For that reason, when asked what the **y-intercept** of a linear equation represents, we will use words like **"initial," "beginning," "starting,"** or indicate that the **independent variable (which usually measures time) is at <u>zero</u>.**

....

Linear word problems will typically present the real world scenario alongside the equation and ask what either the slope or y-intercept represents. If you can memorize what language pairs up with each concept, you can usually arrive at your answer without much understanding of the actual word problem.

Answer choices that contain maximums/minimums or total values are never correct!

Note: You might recall from our earlier discussion of lines that the variables in a linear equation might not always be "x" and "y." Don't be thrown off by different variables. The dependent variable (typically the "y") is the variable that appears alone on one side of the equation. When presented with different variables, take a second to think about which variable acts as the "y" and which one acts as the "x."

Ex:

A phone company calculates its monthly service cost (C) with the following equation. $C = .15m + 30$, where m is the number of minutes a customer uses that month. What does the .15 represent in the equation?

 a) A flat fee for the monthly phone service.

 b) The total number of minutes used by a customer within a month.

 c) The increase in cost for each additional minute used.

 d) The maximum number of minutes a customer can use in a month.

The question is asking us to interpret .15 in the context of the word problem. .15 is the slope of the linear equation *since it modifies the independent variable.* You might remember from earlier that answers that deal with maximums/minimums and/or totals are never correct, so answers (b) and (d) can be immediately eliminated. Answer (a) interprets the meaning of 30 in the equation. 30 was the y-intercept, which is often thought of as an initial value or fixed cost. That leaves us with answer (c). Answer (c) also contains the type of language we would typically look for when we are asked about the slope: "increase," "each," and "additional" are all important terms that help us represent the slope in the context of a real world situation.

....

Occasionally, some of the more challenging linear word problems will require you to be more specific about the slope. **If it's one of the later questions in the section, assume that the increased level of difficulty will require you to determine a more precise relationship between the two variables.** As the independent variable changes by a set amount, what does the dependent variable do? The slope as it appears in the original equation may not be enough to answer a question of this nature. You may have to change both variables proportionally to determine the relationship you are asked about.

Ex:

The equation $p = -.52h + 18.6$ represents the pressure p, in pounds per square foot, exerted on a climber at a height of h feet. What is the increase in height required to decrease the pressure by 1 pound per square foot?

 a) $.52$ feet

 b) 18.6 feet

 c) $\dfrac{1}{.52}$ feet

 d) $\dfrac{1}{18.6}$ feet

You may be able to determine that the important value to consider for this question is -.52. Because the question asked us about the *increase* in height, we are concerned with the slope. Answer choices (b) and (d) both line up with the y-intercept, which is not relevant to the question, so you can eliminate these answer choices.

We need to be precise. We cannot just assume that .52 is the correct answer even though that value will certainly play a role in our answer. Let's start by first determining which variable acts as our "x" and which one acts as our "y": *p* is going to act as our *y* variable, and *h* is going to act as our *x* variable.

Remembering that slope = $\frac{change\ in\ y}{change\ in\ x}$ and representing our slope as a fraction, we can determine that:

$$\frac{-.52}{1} = \frac{\triangle p}{\triangle h}$$

That means the **pressure decreases by .52** pounds per square foot every time the **height increases by 1 foot**. The question wants to know what will cause the pressure to decrease by 1. That will require us to alter the ratio we currently have so that we end up with **-1 in the** *numerator.*

We can do that by dividing the numerator and denominator both by .52.

$$\frac{-.52}{1} \frac{.52}{.52} = \frac{-1}{1/.52}$$

This tells us that the **pressure will decrease by 1** every time the **height increases by** $\frac{1}{.52}$

These questions can be tricky, but if you rely on some of the general test-taking strategies, you can give yourself pretty good odds when guessing. Knowing what language pairs with the y-intercept and what language pairs with slope can usually help you eliminate several answers, like answer choice (b) and answer choice (d). Judging the difficulty of the question by where it falls on the exam can also help you take an educated guess. If this question were found in the final few questions of the section, you should be weary of an answer choice like (a) that simply extracts a number directly from the equation.

. . . .

SYSTEMS OF LINEAR EQUATIONS- MODELING AND POSSIBLE OUTCOMES

While any function or combination of functions (lines, parabolas, circles, etc.) can make up a system of equations, you will mostly encounter *linear* systems. As the name suggests, these are systems made up of two lines. The equations will contain two variables (not always our trusted x and y) and neither variable will be raised to a power bigger than 1.

Before we discuss the possible outcomes for a system of linear equations and the potential methods for solving, let's first discuss how to recognize when a word problem requires a system of equations, and by extension, how to model that system. There are a few major signs to look out for.

1) The word problem is dealing with 2 items/products/services.

2) You are given information about the total *quantity* of items.

3) There is a *value* or *measure* associated with each item: cost, value, weight, capacity, etc.

4) You are given information about the *total* value or measure

If modeled correctly, you will end up with one equation that deals with the <u>quantity</u> of items and one equation that deals with the <u>value</u>.

Ex:

An artist sold small and large prints of her watercolor paintings at a local festival. The small prints were sold for $5 and the large prints were sold for $8. She sold a total of 58 paintings and made $315. How many large paintings were sold?

Let's start by assigning variables that are easy to identify. For the small paintings, we will use the variable "S" and for the large paintings, we will use the variable "L." While we don't know how many of each type she sold, we know that in total, she sold 58. That gives us our first equation.

$$S + L = 58$$

Next, we will deal with the value. Since each small painting costs 5 dollars, to calculate the earnings from small paintings, we will multiply S by 5. In a similar fashion, we will multiply L by 8 to determine the earnings from large paintings. Adding both will produce the total earnings, which we were told was 315 dollars.

$$5S + 8L = 315$$

Some questions may simply ask that you model the system! At this point, your work would be done. Note that you may encounter a similar style of question that requires you to model a system of *inequalities*. The same concepts apply. You will simply have to determine which direction to draw the inequality symbol so that it lines up with the textual information.

Note: Not all systems will give you information about total quantity. Sometimes you will be given a direct relationship between the two variables (one is twice as large as the other, or there is 3 times as much of one product as there is the other). The equations will look a bit different, but there will still be two linear equations involved.

Before we discuss the methods for solving, let's first discuss the possible outcomes for a linear system. This is a concept tested regularly in and of itself. The system will fall into one of these three categories:

1) One solution
2) No solutions
3) Infinite Solutions

You will want to become very familiar with this terminology; **recognition of these phrases will instantly clue you in on the concept being tested**.

A system with **one solution** is made up of **2 distinct lines.** The "solution" to the system is the point at which those two lines intersect.

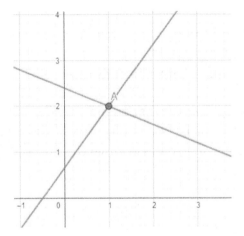

Thinking about this topic visually may help you determine what would cause a system to have **no solutions.** That would be a case where the lines <u>don't intersect</u>. This happens when the **two lines are parallel**. Parallel lines have different y-intercepts, but **identical slopes**.

A question may ask that you design a system so that it has no solutions. This will require you to choose lines that have the same slope.

Ex:

For what value of k will the system of equations below have no solutions?

$$3x + 6y = 8$$
$$kx + 8y = 25$$

The slope of the top equation is -½. This can be determined once the equation is rewritten in *y* = form. That means we need to select a *k* value that would make the slope of the lower equation -½. Let's first get it into *y* = form.

$$y = \frac{-kx}{8} + \frac{25}{8}$$

For *x* to have a coefficient of -½, *k* would need to equal 4.

Questions that test this concept will not always appear as two separate equations stacked on top of one another. You may see one single equation, but the goal is still the same. Treat each side of the equation as its own linear function with its own slope and y-intercept. Then determine whatever missing value would cause the slopes to be equal.

Ex:

For what value of *k* would the following equation have no solutions?

$$4(kx - 3) = 12x - 7$$

To ensure the slopes are equal, the coefficient of both x terms should be equal. If 4*k*=12, *k*=3.

Note: You may have to do a little rearranging to get an equation that looks like the one above. Manipulate the algebra so that you end up with an *x* term on each side. Then you can determine what value would produce equal coefficients.

....

A system with **infinitely many solutions** is one that is made up of the **same line**. The lines may not appear identical at first glance, but if they were to be simplified and/or rearranged, they would be equivalent.

$y = 3x + 4$ does not look like the same equation as $5y - 20 = 15x$, but if we were to get the second into *y* = form we would see that they are in fact identical.

You may have noticed that part of the simplification process was dividing the second equation by 5. That helps to highlight the next point: **one equation is often written as a multiple of the other.** If you are asked to design a system that has **infinite solutions**, that notion will come in handy.

Ex:

For what value of *k* will the system below have infinitely many solutions?

$$2y + 8x = -4$$
$$12y + kx = -24$$

While we can certainly get each equation into *y* = form and compare coefficients, it may be simpler to determine the scale factor (what the first equation was multiplied by to yield the second equation). In this example, we can pretty easily determine that our scale factor was 6.

2 multiplied by 6 gives us 12, and -4 multiplied by 6 gives us -24. That means k would equal 48, the result of multiplying 8 by 6.

....

In summary:

1) One solution: 2 unique lines
2) No solutions: 2 parallel lines -> same slope
3) Infinite solutions: the same line -> one equation is typically a multiple of the other

Be sure you familiarize yourself with these 3 scenarios, the terminology associated with each, and what is required to design a system that produces one solution, no solution, or infinite solutions.

....

SYSTEMS OF LINEAR EQUATIONS- SOLVING

If the system does in fact have a single solution, you may be asked to solve for one or both variables. There are **five ways to solve a first-degree system.**

We will demonstrate the five ways to solve a first-degree system using the following system:

$$2x + 5y = 12$$
$$4x - 3y = -2$$

In addition, we will highlight the scenarios where each method is most useful.

The answer to this system is: **x = 1, y = 2.**

....

METHOD 1: SUBSTITUTION

You can't solve for two variables at once. So, you must find a way to **remove** one variable from a system. This requirement underpins the Substitution and Elimination Methods.

The goal of the substitution method is simple: **replace one variable with an expression that contains the *other* variable.**

Return to the example system. How could this be solved via the substitution method?

$$2x + 5y = 12$$
$$4x - 3y = -2$$

Remember: you're seeking to **substitute one variable with an expression that contains the other variable.** If you could rewrite, say, **y** as an expression that contained **x**, you could find a numerical value for x.

Begin by **isolating y in the first equation, but either variable in either equation could be isolated**:

$$2x + 5y = 12$$
$$-2x \qquad\qquad -2x$$
$$5y = 12 - 2x$$

Dividing by five yields the complete isolation:

$$y = \frac{12}{5} - \frac{2}{5}x$$

You've now created a function for *y* that *contains x.* Return to **the other, unused equation** and **substitute y with that expression. You'll see that only *one variable* remains. This equation can be solved easily, which yields the correct numerical value for x.**

$$4x - 3y = -2$$
$$4x - 3\left(\frac{12}{5} - \frac{2}{5}x\right) = -2$$
$$4x - \frac{36}{5} + \frac{6}{5}x = -2$$
$$\frac{26}{5}x - \frac{36}{5} = -2$$
$$+ \frac{36}{5} \quad + \frac{36}{5}$$
$$\frac{26}{5}x = \frac{26}{5}$$
$$x = 1$$

When you s<u>ubstitute for y, you must remember to use an equation that you haven't used to deter-mine the function for y that was substituted.</u> If you substitute for *y* in the wrong equation, you won't make any progress:

$$2x + 5y = 12$$
$$2x + 5\left(\frac{12}{5} - \frac{2}{5}x\right) = 12$$
$$2x + 12 - 2x = 12$$
$$0 = 0$$

*If you produce this answer, you've likely **substituted for y in the wrong equation.*** Return to the problem and substitute your expression into another equation.

Once you've found a value for *x*, use either equation to calculate the value for *y*:

$$2x + 5y = 12$$
$$2(1) + 5y = 12$$
$$2 + 5y = 12$$
$$\underline{-2 \qquad -2}$$
$$5y = 10$$
$$y = 2$$

The answers are: *x* = 1, *y* = 2.

When it comes to the systems of equations you'll encounter on the SAT, follow these steps to ensure that you execute the substitution method properly:

1) Rewrite one of the equations as a function of one variable.
2) *Substitute* that expression *into the former variable's position* in an unused equation.
3) Solve for one variable.
4) Using either equation and the numerical value of the solved variable, calculate the value of the other variable.

As an exercise, revisit the example system and solve it by **substituting an expression containing *y* into *x*.** If done correctly, this process will produce the same answers.

The substitution method is most useful when one of the variables can be isolated easily, or if one variable has <u>already been isolated</u> in one of the equations. In the example above, isolating *y* gave us an expression that contained fractions. This is not ideal for the non-calculator math section.

....

METHOD 2: ELIMINATION

The addition/elimination method is a second technique that aims to **remove** one of the variables by **adding the two equations together.**

Return to the provided system:

$$2x + 5y = 12$$
$$4x - 3y = -2$$

If we were to add these two equations together (which is allowed), the result would be:

$$2x + 5y = 12$$
$$+ \: (4x - 3y) \: - 2$$
$$6x + 2y = 10$$

You've now produced another equation that seems meaningless, and it's natural at this point to wonder how you could ever use this procedure to *solve* a system of equations. Our goal was to remove one of the variables and adding the two original equations together did not satisfy that goal.

Suppose, however, that you multiply one equation by a factor that creates a coefficient **of equal magnitude but opposite sign** as the coefficient of that same variable in the other equation? **When you add the equations together,** those coefficients will cancel out, **which will** *eliminate one variable* **and let you solve the equation.**

Suppose you wanted to eliminate the x variable from the system. **Multiply the first equation by -2 to yield a -4x:**

$$-2(2x + 5y) = -2(12)$$
$$- \: 4x - 10y = -24$$

Then add this equation to the unused equation. Notice how the x terms "cancel out," leaving only the terms with *y*.

$$-4x - 10y = -24$$
$$+ \: (4x - 3y) = +(-2)$$
$$0x - 13y = -26$$

Calculating a numerical value for *y* yields the correct y = 2.

$$-13y = -26$$
$$y = 2$$

Like in the substitution method, you can plug this value for *y* back into either equation and solve for *x*:

$$2x + 5y = 12$$
$$2x + 5(2) = 12$$
$$2x + 10 = 12$$
$$ - 10 \quad - 10$$
$$2x = 2$$
$$x = 1$$

Follow these steps to ensure that you use the Elimination Method properly:

1) Choose a variable to eliminate.

2) Multiply one equation by a factor that yields a coefficient on the chosen variable that is *the same magnitude* but the *opposite sign* as the coefficient of the same variable in the unused equation.

3) Add the two equations together. The variable that you chose should now have a coefficient of 0, which eliminates it from the problem.

4) Solve for the remaining variable.

5) Using either equation and the numerical value of the solved variable, calculate the value of the other variable.

Practice the elimination method by eliminating *y* in the provided system. If done correctly, you should arrive at the same answer!

The elimination method works best when the factor required to eliminate one variable is a single whole number. Suppose you encountered the following system, with solution x = 2, y = - 3.

$$4x + 3y = -1$$
$$5x + 7y = -11$$

You'll notice that there is **no single, whole number factor that you can use to eliminate one variable.** So, what can you do?

The simplest solution is to **multiply both equations to produce the least common multiple of the two coefficients.** If you wanted to eliminate the *x* term in this system, you'd need to use 20 as the least common multiple. Multiplying the top equation by -5 and the bottom equation by 4 will yield two equations that can be added to eliminate the *x* term. Note that **either equation can include the negative coefficient.**

Many students prefer the elimination method because, if you use least common multiples, you can avoid the fractions that readily arise from the substitution method. If you're uncomfortable with adding fractions, try using the elimination method. Some systems are also primed for the elimination method. One set of variables may already contain opposite coefficients!

Note: For both the substitution and elimination methods, you can smartly choose which variable to **remove** based on the question. If a question asks you to solve for y, remove the x variable. For the elimination method, that would require you to **"cancel" out the y terms.** For the substitution method, you would want to write **x in terms of y,** so that your new equation contained only *y* variables.

....

METHOD 3: GRAPHING THE INTERSECTION

Notice how each equation in the provided system contains a *y* and an *x*. Many systems of equations on the SAT will contain these variables; if not, they'll contain a relationship between *two variables*.

Any function that relates two variables can be graphed on your calculator. So, another way to solve a system of equations is to graph the equations as functions and find the intersection!

Note: If the problem does in fact use variables other than *x* and *y*, just be sure you pay attention to which variable functions as the "*y*" and which one functions as the "*x*."

Rewrite both equations as lines, using standard (*y* = *mx* + *b*) form:

$$2x + 5y = 12$$
$$-2x \qquad\quad -2x$$
$$5y = 12 - 2x$$
$$y = \frac{12}{5} - \frac{2}{5}x$$

And:

$$4x - 3y = -2$$
$$-4x \qquad\quad -4x$$
$$-3y = -2 - 4x$$
$$y = \frac{2}{3} + \frac{4}{3}x$$

Use your graphing calculator to graph these lines, then use either the "intersection" or "table" function to find the intersection! This yields the coordinate (1,2), which provides the correct *x* = 1, *y* = 2 answer.

Follow these steps to graph the intersection correctly:

1) Simplify each equation into "*y* =" form.
2) Graph the equations on your graphing calculator.
3) Use the "intersection" or "table" functions to find the intersection, if it exists.

Note: Graphing is also a useful way to solve systems that include **nonlinear equations**. If you notice a variable with an exponent other than 1 (like quadratics, cubics, or roots), you're dealing with a nonlinear equation. **Graphing the intersection will allow you to solve that system efficiently!**

METHOD 4: PLUGGING IN POINTS

The SAT may sometimes provide coordinate points that offer solutions to the system. This type of question would be formatted like this:

The following system has a solution at:

$$2x + 5y = 12$$
$$4x - 3y = -2$$

a) (3, 4)

b) (1, 2)

c) (-½, 0)

d) (6, 0)

When you're given points as hypothetical solutions to a system of equations, plugging those points back into the equations can be an efficient method to solve the problem, especially if you have your calculator. When you substitute these points back into the equation, ensure that you're plugging the correct value into the correct variable (*x* comes before *y* in most ordered pairs).

You know that Choice (b) is correct, but suppose you didn't. When you start plugging in points, you'd likely begin by plugging the coordinate in Choice (a) back into the first equation. This would allow you to conclude that (3, 4) is not a solution.

Continuing down the answer choices, you'd calculate that Choice (b) satisfies the first equation. Choice (c) doesn't. Choice (d), however, also solves the first equation.

Wait. Choices (b) and (d) both solve the first equation. You know that solutions of linear equations have **one, infinite, or zero solutions**, so how can there be two solutions to a system of linear equations? Well, there can't be. **The SAT will try to trick you by including a point that solves *one equation but not the other*. If you find that a point solves whatever equation you're using, be sure to check that point on the other equation to avoid this trap.**

You'll even notice that both Choice (c) and Choice (b) solve the second equation, but when you check Choice (c) on the first equation, you'll see that it doesn't solve that equation and thus cannot be a solution for the system.

When you encounter a system of equations that gives points as potential solutions, follow these steps:

1) Plug the points back into the equation. Be sure to plug the correct value into the correct variable.

2) If you find that one point satisfies an equation, *check that same point on the other equation to ensure that it's a solution to the system, not just a point on one line.*

....

METHOD 5: MATRIX OPERATIONS

More advanced mathematics students might recognize the potential for matrices to solve systems of equations. If you're uncomfortable or unfamiliar with matrices, you might prefer to use one of the earlier methods. This is a method that is also best utilized on the calculator section, where you can easily perform matrix multiplication.

Start by dividing the example system of equations into three matrices. The first will include the coefficients of your variables. **Be sure that your variables are lined up properly.** The second matrix will include the variables, and the third matrix will include the solutions (or constants):

$$2x + 5y = 12$$
$$4x - 3y = -2$$

This system, in its matrix translation, is:

$$\begin{bmatrix} 2 & 5 \\ 4 & -3 \end{bmatrix} \begin{bmatrix} x \\ y \end{bmatrix} = \begin{bmatrix} 12 \\ -2 \end{bmatrix}$$

Call the coefficient matrix is "A," the variable matrix "X" and the solution matrix "B." This matrix equation then becomes:

$$AX = B$$

To solve for the matrix "X," we need to first determine something called the "inverse matrix." The notation for this is A^{-1}. Applying the inverse matrix to both sides will give us the following equation:

$$X = A^{-1}B$$

The process for multiplying matrices and calculating a matrix's inverse are complex and tedious operations. Lucily your calculator can handle both!

....

If you're using a TI-84, TI-84 Plus CE, or any similar graphing calculator, they're likely equipped with matrix functions. The 2nd option of the x-¹ button takes you to a matrix menu, where you'll see "names," "math," and "edit." To build a matrix, click "edit," select one of the letter matrices, and enter the matrix dimensions (however many rows and columns you need). Once you do that, you can change the values in each cell to match your system.

Create the coefficient and solution matrices in the "edit" menu. **Again, be sure your variables are lined up properly.** When you build the matrices, you must place coefficients of the same variable **on top of each other**. The matrix reads *each column* as belonging to the *same variable*. Similarly, *each row* must include the coefficients and solution of *the same equation*. This is the correct matrix "translation" of the original system:

$$x \begin{bmatrix} 2 & 5 \\ 4 & -3 \end{bmatrix} \begin{bmatrix} x \\ y \end{bmatrix} = \begin{bmatrix} 12 \\ -2 \end{bmatrix} \quad y$$

The following matrix equation, for instance, would be incorrect. Even though they look similar, you should see how two values have been flipped.

$$\begin{bmatrix} 2 & 5 \\ -3 & 4 \end{bmatrix} \begin{bmatrix} x \\ y \end{bmatrix} = \begin{bmatrix} 12 \\ -2 \end{bmatrix}$$

Once you've built the matrices correctly, return to the "names" menu. Select the two matrices that you built and, **after the coefficient matrix, click the "x⁻¹" button**. This will convert the coefficient matrix into its inverse matrix.

Order matters with matrix multiplication, so **you must input the inverse coefficient matrix *followed by the solution matrix.*** If you switch this order, you'll get the wrong answer!

Clicking "enter" will solve the system:

$$\begin{bmatrix} x \\ y \end{bmatrix} = \begin{bmatrix} 2 & 5 \\ 4 & -3 \end{bmatrix}^{-1} \begin{bmatrix} 12 \\ -2 \end{bmatrix}$$
$$\begin{bmatrix} x \\ y \end{bmatrix} = \begin{bmatrix} 1 \\ 2 \end{bmatrix}$$

In summary, if you'd like to use matrices to solve a system of equations, follow these steps:

1) Select "matrix" and "edit." Create a matrix of **coefficients** and a matrix of **solutions**. **Be sure that *coefficients of the same variable* are in the <u>same column</u>, while *each original equation* is in its <u>own row.</u>**

2) Select the coefficient matrix from "names," then hit the "x⁻¹" button to create the inverse matrix. Multiply this inverse matrix by the solution matrix. Since order matters in matrix multiplication, **the inverse of the coefficient matrix must be to the <u>left</u> of the solution matrix.**

Summary:

You've now learned five methods for solving systems of first-degree equations. Some of these methods, like graphing the intersection and plugging in points, are useful when solving systems which include nonlinear equations, too.

You can use substitution and elimination with or without a calculator. Their simplicity and near-universal application tends to make these methods the favorite for most students. Matrix operations and graphing the intersection, while insanely efficient, are best performed with graphing calculators. You can plug in points only for specific question types. As you practice (timed) SAT math sections, apply each of these methods to find which suits you best!

Regardless of your go-to method, <u>**you should always check your answers by plugging them back into each equation in a system. If that checks out, you can be sure that your answer is correct.**</u>

PARABOLAS

After lines, parabolas are the most commonly tested function on the SAT. There are 3 ways to represent the equation of a parabola, and each form of the equation clues us in on different features of the parabola. It is important that you know which properties match up with each form of the equation. The 3 forms are:

- Standard Form
- Factored Form
- Vertex Form

Standard Form is expressed as: $y = ax^2 + bx + c$

From this form of the equation, we can determine 2 features of the parabola.

1) The **direction**. If the leading coefficient "a" is positive, the parabola opens upwards. If "a" is negative, the parabola opens downward.

2) The **y-intercept.** As with any other function, the y-intercept is represented as a constant (the number not attached to a variable). In this case, **the y-intercept is "c."**

Ex: $x^2 + 4x - 12$

Given that "a" is positive, the parabola opens upwards. The y-intercept is (0, -12). We can't determine much else about the graph from this formula. We only know the general shape and that it passes through that single point on the y-axis. The figure shows a couple of possible partial sketches for this parabola.

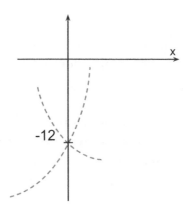

Factored form is expressed as: $y = a(x - n)(x - m)$

From this form of the equation, we can determine 2 features of the parabola.

1) The **direction**. The same rules about the leading coefficient (a) apply.

2) The **zeros**, otherwise known as the **roots** or the **solutions**. They are also the **x-intercepts of the graph. The zeros are "n" and "m."**

Ex: The factored form of the previous example is: $y = (x - 2)(x + 6)$

Given that "a" is positive, we can still determine that the parabola is upwards facing. We can also determine that the zeros/x-intercepts of this parabola are: 2 & -6. The figure below shows a partial sketch of the parabola.

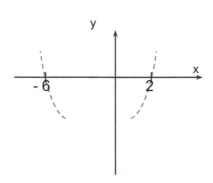

Note: The zeros/x-intercepts end up being the negated values found within each set of parentheses. A factor of (x+6)means the zero will occur at x= -6 and the parabola will cross the x-axis at (-6, 0).

Note: Only quadratics with **REAL** solutions will have x-intercepts. Imaginary solutions do not touch the x-axis.

....

Vertex form is expressed as: $y = a\left(x - h\right)^2 + k$

From this form of the equation, we can determine 2 features of the parabola.

1) The **direction**. The same rules about the leading coefficient (a) apply.
2) The **vertex**. Sometimes referred to as the **maximum/minimum**, the vertex is the point where the parabola changes direction. The **vertex of a parabola is the point (h, k)**.

Ex: The same parabola from the prior examples can be expressed as: $y = (x + 2)^2 - 16$

Once again, we can determine that the parabola is upwards facing, since its leading coefficient is positive. We can also determine that the parabola's vertex will occur at the point (-2,-16). The figure below shows a partial sketch of this parabola.

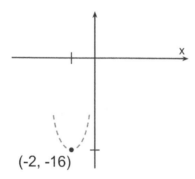

(-2, -16)

Note: The y-coordinate of the vertex is extracted directly from the equation. The x-coordinate gets negated.

....

Vertex form is an incredibly useful form of the parabolic equation. For that reason, you may need to change an equation from its original format *into* vertex form. You can get from standard form to vertex form with a process called **completing the square.**

Step 1: Bring the constant to the other side of the equation.

$$y = x^2 + 4x - 12$$
$$\underline{+12 \qquad\qquad +12}$$
$$y + 12 = x^2 + 4x$$

Step 2: Take the coefficient of the *x* term (the "b"), halve it, and then square it.

$$b = 4 \;\rightarrow\; \left(\frac{4}{2}\right)^2 = 4$$

Step3: Take the result from step 2 and add it to **both** sides of the equation.

$$y + 12 = x^2 + 4x$$
$$\underline{+4 \qquad\quad +4}$$
$$y + 16 = x^2 + 4x + 4$$

Step 4: Factor the right side. You should end up with the same expression in both sets of parentheses. That allows you to rewrite it as *(x-h)²*.

$$y + 16 = x^2 + 4x + 4$$
$$= (x + 2)(x + 2)$$
$$= (x + 2)^2$$

Step 5: Bring the constant back to the other side of the equation.

$$y + 16 = (x + 2)^2$$
$$\underline{-16 \qquad\quad -16}$$
$$y = (x + 2)^2 - 16$$

Note: This process of completing the square is also particularly helpful for problems that deal with the coordinate equation of a circle.

In summary, the 3 forms of the equation for a parabola and the types of information that can be extracted from each are as follows:

- **Standard form: the y-intercept.**

- **Factored form: the x-intercepts/roots/zeros.**

- **Vertex form: the vertex (either a maximum or minimum).**

The direction of the parabola can be found in all three forms of the equation by determining the sign of the leading coefficient.

....

The next few topics are typically found on the calculator portion of the exam. While there is a great deal of overlap between the calculator and non-calculator section, a mastery of these topics will mostly help to improve your performance and boost your level of confidence on the calculator section

STATISTICS AND SURVEY DESIGN

Questions that deal with statistical evidence or surveys will ultimately boil down to two major strategies: **avoiding definitive language** and ensuring that the **sample matches the population.**

The goal of statistics is to study or survey a small group and apply the findings to a much larger group. The small group is called the "sample" and the large group is called the "population." Because it would be inconvenient (and often impossible) to observe or survey all the members of a population, statisticians will use the information regarding the sample to understand the *general* trends in the population. The emphasis here is on the term "general." The population will behave in a *similar* fashion to the sample, but the **values will not be exact**.

That is why will will avoid definitive language that suggests that the findings from the sample study/survey can concretely predict how the population would behave/respond. Avoid language like "all" or "most," and favor words like "plausible," "likely," "roughly," "about."

....

It is also crucial that the population matches the sample **precisely**. If scientists collected data about smallmouth bass in Lake Eerie, they could only use those findings to predict how other smallmouth bass in Lake Eerie would behave — not catfish in Lake Eerie or smallmouth bass in the Mississippi River.

This thinking also applies to surveys. If statisticians wanted to determine how the overall community felt about building a new park, they should not perform the survey at an existing park. The results will not reflect how the **overall** population feels about the construction of a new park. Issues with survey design almost always come down to *where the survey was given and/or who was asked.*

Issues are never in the sample size or population size. The whole purpose of statistics is to apply the findings of a small group on a much larger scale!

....

Some questions may include information about the **margin of error.** The margin of error allows us to determine an *interval* in which the population's data would likely fall. **Adding and subtracting that margin from the initial results** will provide this interval.

If a survey concluded that 54% of the sample was in favor of building a new park, and the margin of error was 3%, we could safely conclude that 51-57% of the population would likely support the new park.

CONDITIONAL PROBABILITY

As a reminder, probability is calculated by creating a ratio of the desired outcomes to the total outcomes. **Conditional probability** calculates the likelihood of an event occuring **after** something has already been decided or after an event has already occured. That initial decision/event is called the "given" condition, and may affect the odds of any future events occuring. The "given" condition will essentially shrink the "universe," or **total** possible outcomes for the future events. Instead of considering **all** of the initial possibilities, you are considering only those that **satisfy the given condition**.

Very often, SAT questions that deal with conditional probability are accompanied by a chart. **A great way to visually "shrink" your universe is to start by circling the row or column that satisfies your given condition.** The total of that specific column/row becomes the denominator of the ratio.

Ex:

Given that a student selected at random is a sophomore, what is the probability that he or she took the ACT only?

	Sophomores	Juniors	Seniors	**Total**
SAT only	88	90	72	250
ACT only	52	45	85	182
SAT and ACT	15	33	20	68
Total	155	168	177	500

The given condition tells us that the student is a sophomore. We would start by circling that row.

	Sophomores	Juniors	Seniors	**Total**
SAT only	88	90	72	250
ACT only	52	45	85	182
SAT and ACT	15	33	20	68
Total	155	168	177	500

The new "total" is the 155 students that fall into that row. This value becomes the denominator. The number of students within that row who took the ACT only becomes the numerator.

$$Probability = \frac{52}{155}$$

SCATTER PLOTS

A scatter plot is a diagram that uses the x-y plane to represent measured values. Those **measured values are represented as points**. If the collection of points follows a particular trend in shape and direction, **a line or curve of best fit** is drawn to visualize the trend. The important thing to remember is that this line or curve simply approximates a general trend and **does NOT represent actual measured values.**

When a problem presents a scatter plot, be sure to think about the difference between the individual points and the line or curve.

- The **points** represent **actual, measured values**.
- Anything that falls on the **line/curve** represents an **estimated or predicted value**.

The scatterplot below represents average flower height for a span of weeks after planting. At 8 weeks, the average flower height would be 19.5 inches, as **indicated by the point**. The *predicted* height would be found by tracing the value associated with the **line**, in this case 18.

If asked to find *the equation* of the line of best fit, treat it as any other linear graph problem. Focus on identifying the slope and the y-intercept. To calculate slope, you will need to extract two points from the graph. Pick points that **fall near a corner on the grid-lines.**

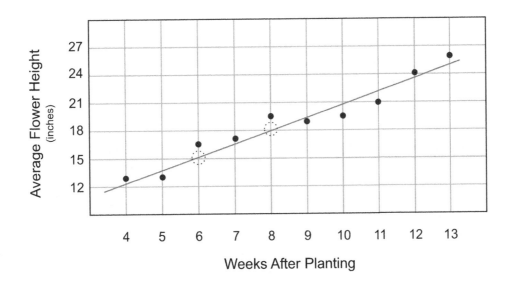

In this example, the points (6, 15) and (8, 18) are useful, since they fall very close to the grid-lines.

Note: Be very detail-oriented when determining the equation of a line presented on a graph, whether the graph is associated with a scatter plot or not. **Pay close attention to the axis labels**; do not assume that one "box" represents one unit. Also **pay close attention to where the graph "begins."** The axes do not always start at 0, so making that assumption could lead you to estimate the y-intercept incorrectly. To avoid these traps, focus on the actual points that you extracted from the line and use those values to build the equation formulaically. Don't try to simply "observe" the features of the line.

QUESTION-SPECIFIC TIPS

These next few pages will focus on tips you can apply to very specific question-types. They will also review certain identifying phrases built into the question that can help you pinpoint the underlying topic and the proper approach.

EQUATIONS CONTAINING RADICALS

Simple equations that contain radicals can be dealt with algebraically, but when the answer choices suggest that there are **multiple possible solutions, your approach should change**. If the answers are in **set notation** (where one or more answers are included in a set of braces {a,b}), or the question is constructed in a way that you can **select more than one value**, you should __NOT solve the equation algebraically__.

Why? When you solve an equation that contains a radical, you must check your solutions. But since the SAT expects that students will not check their solutions, one of the solutions will probably not work when it's plugged back into the original equations. Because radicals behave in this way, it is *crucial* to check all possible solutions. For that reason, it's smarter (and way faster) to do that from the start! **Do not default to working through the algebra; simply plug in the possible answers and determine which values (typically only one will work) give you a true statement.**

Ex:

What is the set of all solutions to the equation $\sqrt{x+6} = x$?

a) $\{-2,3\}$

b) $\{0\}$

c) $\{3\}$

d) $\{-2\}$

It's no coincidence that we see -2 & 3 together in answer (a) and separately in answers (c) and (d). If we were to solve this equation by hand, we would end up with a quadratic that yielded those two values as solutions. But once we checked both solutions by plugging them into the equation, we'd see that -2 does not work.

$$\sqrt{(3)+6} = (3) \qquad \sqrt{(-2)+6} = (-2)$$
$$\sqrt{9} = 3 \qquad \sqrt{4} = -2$$
$$3 = 3 \checkmark \qquad 2 = -2 \otimes$$

The easiest and fastest way to solve this problem would have been to plug in both of those values without handling the algebra and solving the quadratic.

For problems that provide only one possible solution at a time, you may still want to consider "solving" these problems simply by plugging in the answers. Start by plugging in the values that would <u>give you easy square roots to calculate</u>, especially on the non-calculator section.

Ex:

What value of k will satisfy the equation below?

$$\sqrt{k-3} + 5 = k$$

    a) 4

    b) 7

    c) 8

    d) 10

Plugging in values like 8 or 10 would give us impossible square roots to calculate ($\sqrt{5}$ and $\sqrt{7}$). Both of these values *exist*, but they are not whole numbers and we can not calculate them by hand. These irrational square roots are likely incorrect. Plugging in values like 4 and 7 would give us much more manageable numbers, as we would be calculating $\sqrt{1}$ and $\sqrt{4}$. Ultimately, answer (b) would be our answer.

SINES AND COSINES OF COMPLEMENTARY ANGLES

Trigonometry as a whole is not a heavily tested concept on the SAT. Using the sides of a right triangle to determine the sine, cosine, or tangent of an angle may pop up on occasion. Simply memorizing the ratios for each trig function (remembering **SohCahToa** is particularly useful) is enough to get you through a bulk of those problems. These ratios can be found on the formula sheet at the end of the chapter.

Beyond that, the only trigonometric concept that is tested regularly is the following rule: **when two angles are complementary — meaning they add up to 90 degrees — the sine of one angle equals the cosine of the other.** This concept gets tested most often on the grid-in section.

<u>When you are given information about sine and cosine in a single problem, you can almost guarantee this is the concept being tested and that the sine and cosine are equal to one another.</u> If you want to be sure, look for information that would indicate the two angles in question are **complementary**.

Ex:

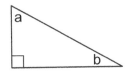

If sin(a) = .4, what is cos(b)?

Given the nature of the question, we can pretty reasonably assume the trigonometric rule discussed earlier is what is being tested. But to be sure, we should try to determine if these two angles are complements of one another. While we don't know their exact values, they are the two acute angles in a right triangle. That means they have to add up to 90 degrees. **Since they are complementary angles, the sine of one equals the cosine of the other**. Since the sine of angle a is .4, the cosine of angle b is also .4.

The previous example didn't require much actual math. For that reason, these questions are usually fairly simple if you can <u>nail down the rule</u> and **recognize when it's being tested.**

SOLVING FOR AN EXPRESSION

You may find that some questions ask that you solve for an *expression*. As a reminder, a mathematical expression is a collection of terms (variables and/or numbers) with at least one operation (like addition or subtraction). 5x+3y is an example of an expression. If you are asked to solve for an expression of this nature, it's very likely that a shortcut is built into the question.

You may be tempted to solve for *x*, then solve for *y*, and plug both of those values into the expression to determine its value. While that approach isn't *wrong*, it can be time consuming and prone to careless mistakes, especially when you are not permitted your calculator.

So what can we do? We can try to solve for 5*x*+3*y* **as a unit**, not as a combination of its smaller components. Many times, there are ways to manipulate the algebra so that you end up with an equation 5*x* + 3*y* = some value.

How to manipulate the algebra will depend on the specific question. When presented with a **system of equations**, try not to default to the traditional approach. Try instead to add the two equations together **exactly as they are**. That operation alone may give you your answer.

Ex:

What is the value of 6*x*- 6*y* given that:

$$4x - 2y = 1000$$
$$2x - 4y = 1200$$

If we were to add these two equations together, we would end up with the following:

$$\begin{array}{r} 4x - 2y = 1000 \\ +\ 2x - 4y = 1200 \\ \hline 6x - 6y = 2200 \end{array}$$

We end up with an equation that provides the value for 6x-6y instantly. We also saved ourselves a lot of time and effort by not solving the entire system.

You may find that an extra step is necessary after adding the equations together, like factoring. Even with the extra step, the process is still far quicker and simpler than solving for the separate variables.

Ex:

If $2x - 8y = 12$ and $3x - 2y = 13$, what is the value of $x - 2y$?

Again, start by adding the equations together.

$$\begin{aligned} 2x - 8y &= 12 \\ + \quad 3x - 2y &= 13 \\ \hline 5x - 10y &= 25 \end{aligned}$$

We do not have an equation that contains *x-2y* directly— yet! By simply factoring out a 5, we will end up with:

$$5(x - 2y) = 25$$

We can now solve for *x-2y* as a whole, by dividing out the 5. We are treating *x-2y* almost as if it's a variable.

$$\frac{5(x-2y)}{5} = \frac{25}{5}$$

$$x - 2y = 5$$

Note: Thinking of an expression as a variable can be a helpful tool for other problems where the same expression appears multiple times in an equation or larger expression. You may find that renaming the expression can help you manipulate the algebra more easily. Replace the expression with the variable of your choosing anywhere it appears in the original equation/expression and work through the algebra. When you are finished, replace the variable with the expression you renamed.

POLYNOMIAL LONG DIVISION

Several questions on the exam will ask that you rewrite an expression to find an **equivalent form**. You might remember from the strategy chapter that it's important to start manipulating the expression/ equation **any way that you can**. The core four methods of rewriting an expression are: factoring, distributing, expanding, and combining like terms. Those techniques can work for any number of equations or expressions.

Beyond that, there are a few techniques that only apply to certain expressions/equations, like cross multiplying. That will only work for an *equation* that has a *fraction* on one or both sides.

Another key method for rewriting a rational expression (a fraction in which numerator and denominator are made up of polynomials) is **polynomial long division**. Once practiced, the process itself is not all that challenging. The difficulty is recognizing *when* to use it. There are two major signs.

1) When there is nothing else that can be done to the expression and/or factoring does not help us to simplify

2) When one or more answer choices contains a term that looks like a **remainder**.

The second clue is perhaps the most obvious. If one or more of your answer choices contains a **fraction written over the <u>original denominator</u>**, that is the **remainder**. That tells us that long division is necessary.

Ex:

The expression $\dfrac{6x - 7}{x - 2}$ is equivalent to which of the following:

a) $6 + \dfrac{7}{2}$

b) $\dfrac{6 - 7}{2}$

c) $6 - \dfrac{19}{x - 2}$

d) $6 + \dfrac{5}{x - 2}$

Answer choices (c) and (d) provide us the biggest clues that polynomial long division is necessary, as they both contain terms that look like remainders. Answer (a) and (b) also attempt to simplify the expression in ways that are not mathematically legitimate. We cannot cancel the x out of numerator and denominator as answer choice (b) suggests. And we cannot split the fraction down the middle and simplify as answer choice (a) suggests.

The process for polynomial long division is directly related to traditional long division, which is discussed in a later chapter.

The process for polynomial long division is shown below.

$$x - 2 \overline{) 6x - 7}$$

Determine how many times x goes into $6x$.

$$x - 2 \overline{) 6x - 7}^{\,6}$$

Place the result on top. Then multiply the result by each term outside the radical.

$$x - 2 \overline{) \begin{array}{c} 6 \\ 6x - 7 \\ 6x - 12 \end{array}}$$

Place your results under the corresponding terms beneath the radical.

$$x - 2 \overline{) \begin{array}{c} 6 \\ 6x - 7 \\ - (6x - 12) \\ \hline 5 \end{array}}$$

Subtract the results from the corresponding terms. You may want to use parentheses to ensure you subtract **each** term.

Bring any remaining terms down and repeat the process if necessary. When division is no longer possible, the result is your **remainder**. **Place that term over the <u>original denominator.</u>**

Answer: $6 + \dfrac{5}{x-2}$

While this topic may not appear as regularly as some of the other topics we have discussed, recognition of the concept being tested can go a long way in helping you take an educated guess. Eliminating the answers that break the rules of math (like answers (a) and (b) in the example above) and knowing to select a term with a remainder for similar looking questions will give you much better odds when guessing.

USING A CONJUGATE

Another form of algebraic manipulation that can be applied to *specific* rational expressions is **multiplication by a conjugate**. The **conjugate** of a two-term expression is simply the <u>**same expression with the opposite sign in the middle**</u>. For example, the conjugate of *x*-4 would be *x*+4.

Similar to polynomial long division, the trick is to determine *when* multiplication by a conjugate is necessary. The biggest clue of all is when we see an <u>**imaginary number (i)**</u> or a <u>**radical**</u> in the rational expression. We can alter the rational expression by multiplying the top and bottom by the **conjugate of the <u>DENOMINATOR</u>.**

This process will **eliminate** the imaginary terms and/or radicals in the denominator. Before we attempt to rewrite an entire rational expression, let's first observe *how* this elimination process works.

$$(2 + \sqrt{3})(2 - \sqrt{3})$$

$$(2)(2) + (2)(-\sqrt{3}) + (\sqrt{3})(2) + (\sqrt{3})(-\sqrt{3})$$

$$4 - 2\sqrt{3} + 2\sqrt{3} - 3$$

$$4 - 3 = 1$$

Note: A radical multiplied by itself will eliminate the radical and leave only what was underneath.

$$(2 - 3i)(2 + 3i)$$

$$(2)(2) + (2)(3i) + (-3i)(2) + (-3i)(3i)$$

$$4 + 6i - 6i - 9i^2$$

$$4 - 9i^2$$

$$4 - 9(-1) \longrightarrow 4 + 9 = 13$$

Note: i^2 is equal to -1.

Ex:

The expression $\dfrac{4-3i}{6+2i}$ is equivalent to which of the following:

a) $\dfrac{4}{6} - \dfrac{3i}{2i}$

b) $\dfrac{4}{6} + \dfrac{3i}{2i}$

c) $\dfrac{9}{20} + \dfrac{13i}{20}$

d) $\dfrac{9}{20} - \dfrac{13i}{20}$

Just as we saw with the example for polynomial long division, two of the answers attempt to simplify the expression in ways that are not mathematically legitimate. Answers (a) and (b) both attempt to split the fraction down the middle, which is not allowed. Eliminating those two choices for breaking a fundamental rule of math narrows down the options significantly.

Deciding between answers (c) and (d) will require us to multiply the numerator and denominator of the original expression by the conjugate of the denominator.

$$\dfrac{4-3i}{6+2i} \cdot \dfrac{(6-2i)}{(6-2i)} \longrightarrow \dfrac{(4)(6)+(4)(-2i)+(-3i)(6)+(-3i)(-2i)}{(6)(6)+(6)(-2i)+(2i)(6)+(2i)(-2i)}$$

$$\dfrac{24-8i-18i+6i^2}{36-4i^2} = \dfrac{24-26i-6}{36+4} = \dfrac{18-26i}{40}$$

At this point, we can <u>split the rational expression into two separate fractions by giving each term in the numerator its OWN denominator</u>. We will want to keep the original operation from the numerator (in this case, subtraction). We can then simplify each fraction separately.

$$\dfrac{18-26i}{40} \longrightarrow \dfrac{18}{40} - \dfrac{26i}{40}$$

$$= \dfrac{9}{20} - \dfrac{13i}{20}$$

PERFORMING BASIC OPERATIONS BY HAND

One of the best ways to avoid careless mistakes on this section is to practice performing basic arithmetic by hand. It may seem silly, but it's probably been a while since you've had to perform basic operations without the use of your calculator. You want to be able to do these calculations quickly and comfortably. We will focus on some of the slightly trickier concepts or those that are prone to careless mistakes.

ADDING AND SUBTRACTING

Adding two positive numbers is simple enough, but when you are combining a negative value with a positive value, things can get a bit messy. First things first, adding a negative is the same thing as subtracting.

-17 + 23   is the same thing as   23 - 17

Let's review the two traditional methods of subtraction. You will start by placing the number you are subtracting underneath the number you are subtracting from. You will then move from right to left, subtracting one column at a time . When the number on top is smaller than the number on the bottom, you must "borrow" from the next column. Here are two ways of doing that:

$$
\begin{array}{r}
\overset{\overset{12}{}}{7\cancel{2}} \\
-\,\overset{4}{\cancel{3}}5 \\
\hline
37
\end{array}
\qquad\qquad
\begin{array}{r}
\overset{6\ \ 12}{\cancel{7}\cancel{2}} \\
-\,3\,5 \\
\hline
3\,7
\end{array}
$$

Things get even trickier when we are subtracting a larger number from a smaller number. Here's the simplest way of handling the operation.

1) Subtract the "smaller" number from the "larger" number (think only about absolute values here and ignore positives/negatives)

2) Take the sign of the "larger" number

$$\text{Ex: } -53 + 18 \quad\text{OR}\quad 18 - 53 \longrightarrow \begin{array}{r} 5\,3 \\ -\,1\,8 \\ \hline 3\,5 \end{array} \longrightarrow -35$$

Since -53 had the larger absolute value, we took the negative sign, which made our answer -35.

···

Subtracting a negative is the same thing as adding.

$12 - (-7)$ is the same thing as $12 + 7$

···

ADDING AND SUBTRACTING FRACTIONS

When adding or subtracting fractions, you need to **establish a common denominator** so that each fraction is "over" the same number. To find the common denominator between two fractions, calculate a **common multiple of each denominator**.

A common multiple of a set of numbers is a number that is **divisible** by each of the numbers in the set. The most common of the common multiples (try that tongue-twister!) is the *least* **common multiple. The least common multiple of a set of numbers is the *smallest* number that is divisible by the numbers of the set**. So, for example, the least common multiple of 5 and 4 is 20, since 20 is the smallest number that has both 5 and 4 as factors. The least common multiple of 2 and 3 is 6 for the same reason.

Identifying the least common multiple can be tricky at times, but one method that allows you to calculate a common multiple is to **multiply both numbers together.** For instance, if you want to find a common multiple of 10 and 2, you can use 20, which is what you'll get when you multiply 10 by 2. Even though 10 is the least common multiple (since 10 is the smallest number that is divisible by 10 and 2), you can just as easily use 20 as your common multiple.

Suppose we have the following fraction addition:

$$\frac{4}{5} + \frac{2}{3}$$

The denominators are **5** and **3**. Multiplying 5 by 3, you can calculate a common multiple of 15, which is also the least common multiple of those two numbers. So what's next once you've determined the common multiple?

You will then need to **modify each fraction so that its denominator becomes the common denominator**. Figure out what you'd need to multiply the current denominator by to yield the common denominator. **Then multiply numerator *and* denominator by that value.** In the same way we can't do something to one side of an equation without doing it to the other side, we can't alter one part of the fraction without altering the other.

Returning to the example, the denominator of the first fraction would need to be multiplied by 3, since 5 x 3 will give us 15. We must also multiply the numerator by 3 to "balance" the fraction. Similarly, for the second fraction, we multiply numerator and denominator both by 5, since that 3 x 5 will give us 15.

$$\left(\frac{3}{3}\right)\frac{4}{5} + \frac{2}{3}\left(\frac{5}{5}\right) \longrightarrow \frac{12}{15} + \frac{10}{15}$$

You may only add fractions if they have a common denominator. Thus, once you've calculated the common denominator, add the numerators and place your answer over the common denominator to yield the correct answer. Be sure to simplify the resulting fraction, if possible:

$$\frac{12}{15} + \frac{10}{15} = \frac{22}{15}$$

The following steps summarize how to add or subtract fractions:

1) **Identify a common denominator.** The common denominator can be calculated by finding the least common multiple of the set of denominators, or, if the least common multiple isn't obvious, by multiplying the set of denominators together.

2) **"Balance" each fraction.** Multiply each numerator by the same factor needed to transform that denominator into the common denominator.

3) **Add the numerators and preserve the common denominator.**

4) **Simplify the fraction, if possible.**

....

LONG DIVISION

Let's begin with a reminder of what to call each of the numbers in a division problem. We'll begin by examining this fraction:

$$\frac{13}{5}$$

When approaching a long division problem, it's important to identify two numbers. Firstly, identify the **dividend**. The **dividend** is the number that's **"being divided."** When you're presented with a fraction, the dividend is always the numerator. Then, identify the **divisor**. The **divisor** is the number that's **"doing the dividing."** In a fraction, the divisor is always the denominator. Once you've identified the dividend and divisor, arrange them around the long division sign, like this:

$$divisor\overline{)dividend}^{quotient}$$

Note that the "quotient" is the answer to the division problem. So, for the provided fraction, you'd find:

$$5\overline{)13}$$

Once you've accurately identified the divisor and dividend, you're ready to divide.

You'll always want to ask yourself how many "times" the divisor can fit into a given part of the dividend. **Proceed, digit by digit, through the dividend**. How many times will "5" fit into 1? Well, 0. But what about "13"? 2 times, with 3 left over.

Once you've found that the divisor can be divided into the dividend a non-zero amount of times, write that number in the quotient above the digit in the dividend that allows you to perform that division. Then, multiply that number by the divisor, and subtract that product from the dividend:

$$
\begin{array}{r}
2 \\
\hline
5\overline{)13} \\
-10 \\
\hline
3
\end{array}
$$

See how you've calculated a 3? **Since 5 doesn't go into 3, you'll have to drag down the next digit in 13.** But what's the next digit in 13? Haven't you used all of them? Well, no. **Drag down a 0** from 13, because 13 is really 13.000000..., and continue dividing. <u>Since you accessed the decimal place, be sure to move the decimal point directly up to the **corresponding** place in the quotient.</u>

Continue with your division by asking how many times 5 goes into 30 (3 "plus" the extra 0). That yields 6, which, when multiplied by 5 and subtracted from 30, produces 0:

$$
\begin{array}{r}
2.6 \\
\hline
5\overline{)13.0} \\
-10 \\
\hline
30 \\
-30 \\
\hline
0
\end{array}
$$

Producing a 0 stops the division. You might have to continue a few more times before you find a 0. You may also find repeating decimals, so if you notice a pattern, you might be dealing with a repeating decimal and you may stop dividing.

In summary, follow these steps to perform long division by hand effectively:

1) Identify the **divisor** and **dividend**. Arrange them correctly around the division sign.

2) Check how many times the divisor "goes into" each digit of the dividend.

3) Multiply that number by the divisor. Subtract that product from the dividend.

4) Drag down the next digit in the dividend, and check how many times the divisor "goes into" that number.

5) If you access the decimal point, drag down a 0 for every subsequent division, and be sure to move the decimal point to the corresponding place in the quotient.

6) Stop when a 0 is produced after subtraction, or when you find a repeating pattern.

....

MULTIPLYING AND DIVIDING FRACTIONS

Multiplying fractions is much easier than adding fractions. To multiply fractions, you simply multiply across:

$$\frac{4}{5} \cdot \frac{2}{3} = \frac{8}{15}$$

You can see that 4 x 2 = 8, and 5 x 3 = 15.

One helpful trick when multiplying fractions is to "cross-eliminate." Suppose you multiplied the following fractions:

$$\frac{4}{7} \cdot \frac{1}{2} = \frac{4}{14} = \frac{2}{7}$$

By multiplying across, you'd calculate: 4 x 1 = 4 and 7 x 2 = 14. However, you'll notice that you would need to simplify to arrive at the correct answer. Cross-elimination allows you to "skip" the unsimplified intermediate and directly produce the simplified answer.

Notice how a factor of 2 was "removed" to simplify the intermediate fraction. Look at the original fractions. Notice how one has a numerator of 4, and the other has a denominator of 2. 4 divided by 2 is 2. That's where the hidden 2 comes from!

To cross-eliminate, you should i**dentify numbers that have common factors across the multiplication sign.** <u>**One must be a numerator, and the other must be a denominator, but the values do NOT have to belong to the same fraction.**</u> Simplify each term by dividing them each by their common factor.

$$\frac{④}{7} \cdot \frac{1}{②} = \frac{2}{7} \cdot \frac{1}{1} = \frac{2}{7}$$

If you decide not to cross-eliminate, you'll still arrive at the right answer, but you'll need to simplify your end result.

These steps will allow you to multiply fractions effectively:

1) Look for any factors that you can cross-eliminate.

2) Multiply across.

3) Simplify the fraction, if possible.

....

Division can be thought of as multiplication by the <u>reciprocal</u>. The reciprocal of a **whole number is 1 divided by that number.** The reciprocal of a **fraction is simply the "flip" of that fraction,** where numerator and denominator are swapped.

When dividing fractions, simply **multiply the first by the reciprocal of the second (or the numerator by the reciprocal of the denominator)**:

$$\frac{4}{7} \div \frac{1}{2} = \frac{4}{7} \cdot \frac{2}{1} = \frac{8}{7}$$

Note: You can use everything you know about multiplying fractions when dividing. Once you've identified the reciprocal, check to see if you can cross-eliminate any factors and then multiply across.

Here are the steps you should follow to divide fractions correctly:

1) Identify the reciprocal of the fraction that sits after the division sign (or the one in the denominator of the original expression).

2) Multiply the original fraction and that reciprocal. Apply what you know about fraction multiplication.

....

MULTIPLYING AND DIVIDING DECIMALS

Some of the trickiest operations are those that involve decimals. Let's begin with a review of multiplication. The best way to tackle decimal multiplication is to follow these steps:

1) Count up how many decimal places you have in **both** numbers. This is determined by counting how many digits are on the **right** side of the decimal (for example, 6.245 has 3 decimal places).

2) Multiply the two numbers normally, ignoring the decimal points.

3) **After** your calculations, place the decimal point in your answer. Your answer should have **the same number of decimal places found in step 1**.

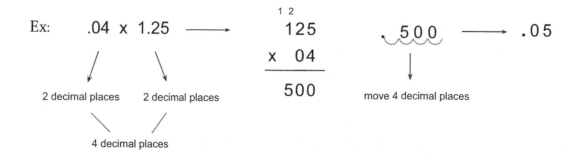

....

Finally, let's discuss how to divide decimals. This is best explained through an example:

$$\frac{14.4}{.12}$$

The appearance of the decimals in a fraction may seem awkward and you're not wrong to feel that way. We can "fix" the issue by manipulating the ratio so that it no longer contains any decimals. Remember that we are allowed to multiply fractions by a scale factor <u>as long as we multiply both numerator and denominator by the same value.</u>

Multiplying the numerator and denominator by 10 will move the decimal point of each to the right one digit. That would yield:

$$\frac{14.4\,(10)}{.12\,(10)} = \frac{144}{1.2}$$

Doing this one more time will eliminate the decimals entirely and give us a much simpler operation to perform:

$$\frac{144\,(10)}{1.2\,(10)} = \frac{1440}{12}$$

FORMULA SHEET

Given Formulas

$A = \pi r^2$ $A = \ell w$ $A = \frac{1}{2}bh$ $c^2 = a^2 + b^2$ Special Right Triangles

$C = 2\pi r$

$V = \ell wh$ $V = \pi r^2 h$ $V = \frac{4}{3}\pi r^3$ $V = \frac{1}{3}\pi r^2 h$ $V = \frac{1}{3}\ell wh$

The number of degrees of arc in a circle is 360.
The number of radians of arc in a circle is 2π.
The sum of the measures in degrees of the angles of a triangle is 180.

Trigonometry

$$sin(x) = \frac{Opposite}{Hypotenuse}$$

$$cos(x) = \frac{Adjacent}{Hypotenuse}$$

$$tan(x) = \frac{Opposite}{Adjacent}$$

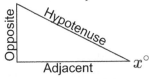

If $a + b = 90° \rightarrow sin(a) = cos(b)$

$$sin^2(x) + cos^2(x) = 1$$

Properties of Lines

$$y = mx + b$$

where *m* is slope and *b* is the y-intercept

$$Slope\ (m) = \frac{change\ in\ y}{change\ in\ x} = \frac{rise}{run} = \frac{y_1 - y_2}{x_1 - x_2}$$

$$Midpoint = \left(\frac{x_1 + x_2}{2}, \frac{y_1 + y_2}{2}\right)$$

$$Distance = \sqrt{(x_1 - x_2)^2 + (y_1 - y_2)^2}$$

Parallel lines have equal slopes
Perpendicular lines have slopes that are negative reciprocals

Factoring and Quadratics

Factoring Identities

$$x^2 - y^2 = (x - y)(x + y)$$
$$x^2 + 2xy + y^2 = (x + y)^2$$
$$x^2 - 2xy + y^2 = (x - y)^2$$

Completing the Square:
1) Bring all constants to one side of equation
2) Take b term and divide by 2
3) Square that value and add result to both sides of equation
4) Factor new quadratic as $(x + \frac{b}{2})^2$
5) Move constants back to other side

Quadratic Formula:
$$x = \frac{-b \pm \sqrt{b^2 - 4ac}}{2a}$$

If discriminant $\sqrt{b^2 - 4ac}$ is:
- zero: one real solution
- positive: two real solutions
- negative: two imaginary solutions

All polynomials p(x) are divisible by (x-k) if k is a zero

When converting:
From larger unit to smaller unit: **multiply**
From smaller unit to larger unit: **divide**

Conics

Circles

$$(x - h)^2 + (y - k)^2 = r^2$$

where (h,k) is center and r is the radius

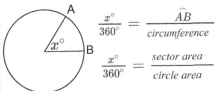

$$\frac{x°}{360°} = \frac{\overset{\frown}{AB}}{circumference}$$

$$\frac{x°}{360°} = \frac{sector\ area}{circle\ area}$$

Parabolas

$$y = (x - h)^2 + k$$
where (h,k) is the vertex

$$y = ax^2 + bx + c$$
where c is the y-intercept

$$y = (x - n)(x - m)$$
where n,m are the zeros (x-intercepts)

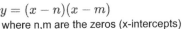

Angle/Triangle Properties

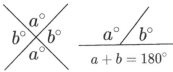

$$a + b = 180°$$

Angles in a triangle add up to $180°$
Angles **opposite** congruent sides are congruent

Similar triangles have congruent angles and proportional side lengths

$$a^2 + b^2 = c^2$$

Special Right Triangles:
3 - 4 - 5
5 - 12 - 13
*and multiples of each

Exponents

$$a^x a^y = a^{x+y}$$
$$(a^x)^y = a^{xy}$$
$$a^{\frac{x}{y}} = \sqrt[y]{a^x}$$
$$\frac{a^x}{a^y} = a^{x-y}$$
$$a^{-x} = \frac{1}{a^x}$$
$$a^0 = 1$$

Additional Topics/Formulas

$$Distance = speed \times time$$

$$Total\ cost = cost\ per\ unit \times \#\ of\ units$$
(cost/price/weight/volume/area)

$$Average \atop (Mean) = \frac{Sum}{\#\ of\ terms}$$

Median: middle value in ordered set
Mode: most occuring value in set

$$Percent\ Change = \frac{Ending - Initial}{Initial} \times 100$$

$$A = P(1 \pm \frac{r}{n})^{nt}$$
A=amount, P= initial amount, r=rate, n=compounding per year, t=years

Complex number: *a + bi*
$$i = \sqrt{-1} \qquad i^2 = -1$$

Systems of Linear Equations:
- have **one** solution (x,y) when two distinct lines intersect
- have **no** solutions when lines are parallel
- have **infinite** solutions when the lines are the same (one is a multiple of the other)
- can be solved graphically, with substitution, or with addition/elimination method

HOW TO GRID IN YOUR RESPONSES

Both the non-calculator and calculator math sections end with "grid-in" questions. Much like when you fill in your name on the answer sheet, you'll be asked to write in numbers above a column of corresponding bubbles. You may recognize the blank grid-in box pictured here. Notice how the box begins with two fraction bars and four decimal points — this suggests that some answers may be fractions or decimals.

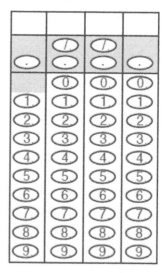

While it may seem like this box is just a box, **its structure lends itself to a few strategies that may reveal if you've made a mistake in your math**. Keep the following tips in mind.

....

You can't grid in a negative. Look again at the sample grid-in box. *There isn't an option to bubble in a negative sign*. So if your response is a negative number, you've made a mistake. Revisit the problem and check your work. It's likely that you missed a negative sign somewhere, so pay special attention to any negative signs that you use in your calculations.

Similarly, you've probably noticed that there are only four bubbles. So what do you do if you have a number with more than four digits, like .6666666...? Firstly, you should **prefer fractions over decimals whenever possible**; finite decimals like .5 can be written as ½. Repeating decimals like .666666... can be rewritten as ⅔. It's probably safer to grid in your response as a fraction, but if you prefer to grid in a repeating decimal, **you must use all four boxes**. Circling back to the previous example, .66 would <u>not</u> be accepted. Either .666 or .667 would be acceptable responses, as they utilize all four grid-in boxes.

Be sure to always simplify your fractions! You should also make sure to convert any mixed numbers into fractions (or, if you prefer, decimals). 1½, for example, cannot be gridded in as: [1][1][/][2]. You could either grid it in as 1.5 or 3/2.

So what happens if you calculate a response with more than four digits that can't be easily converted into a fraction? Most questions with a non-terminating, non-repeating decimal answer would **ask you to round** to a specific decimal place. **But if the question *doesn't* instruct you to round to a certain digit, and your response is a non-terminating, non-repeating decimal, then you've probably made a mistake.** The "standardized" design of the SAT prohibits any ambiguity, so responses that could be debated (should you round to the hundredths or thousandths place?) are always wrong. Note that you're most likely to come across this situation on the calculator section, since answers with long decimals typically don't appear on the non-calculator section.

CALCULATOR TIPS AND TRICKS

First thing's first, let's talk about which calculators you are permitted to use. Most of you are using some form of a TI-83 or TI-84, which is allowed. Although a graphing calculator isn't necessary, it is an incredibly useful tool. If you were planning on using a scientific calculator, strongly consider upgrading to a calculator with a graphing component. The TI-84 Plus CE is a great option. Check out curvebreakerstestprep.com for some detailed blog posts discussing calculators.

Below is a list of all of the devices that are **NOT** permitted for the SAT exam.

- Laptops or other computers, tablets, cell phones, or smartphones
- Smartwatches or wearable technology of any kind
- Models that can access the Internet, have wireless, Bluetooth, cellular, audio/video recording and playing, camera, or any other smart phone type feature
- Models that have a computer-style (QWERTY) keypad, pen-input, or stylus
- Models that use electrical outlets, make noise, or have a paper tape
- Calculator function on a mobile phone
- In addition, the use of hardware peripherals such as a stylus with an approved calculator is not permitted. Some models with touch-screen capability are not permitted (e.g., Casio ClassPad).

....

Now that that's settled, let's discuss some functions of the calculator.

Inputting a Fraction

1) Press "alpha"
2) Press "y="
3) 3) Press "enter" to select "1:n/d"

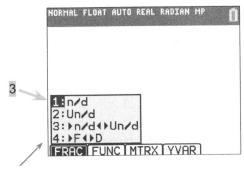

NOTE: There are several other function you'll see in this list.
"2: Un/d" will allow you to input a mixed number
"3: ▶n/d ◀ ▶ Un/d" will change a fraction into a mixed number

To get a decimal in fraction form:

1) Press "math"

2) Press "enter" to select "1: ▸ Frac"

3) Press "enter"

* To get from fraction form into decimal, repeat the procedure, but select "2: Dec"

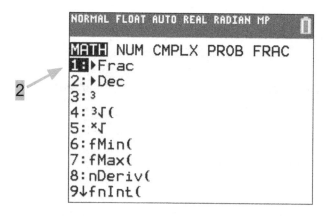

To determine the factors of a number

1) Press "y="

2) Input that number divided by x into Y1

3) Press "2ND" and then "graph" to bring you to the table

4) Any x-y pairs that are whole numbers are factors of that initial value

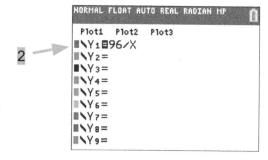

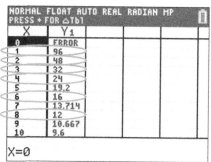

To find a zero (solution or root) by graphing

1) Press "y="

2) Input function into Y1=

3) Press "graph" (the graph will appear in your window; if it does not, try zooming out by pressing "zoom" and scrolling down to "3: zoom out")

4) Press "2ND" and then "trace"

5) Scroll down to "2: zero" and press "enter"

6) Move the cursor to a spot on the curve to the LEFT of the zero. Push "enter"

7) Move the cursor to a spot on the curve to the RIGHT of the zero. Push "enter"

8) Push "enter" a third time

9) The x and y coordinates will appear at the bottom of the screen

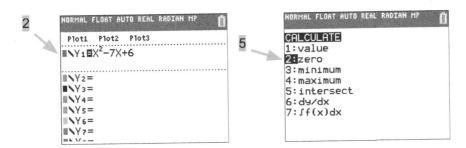

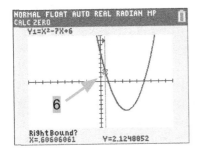

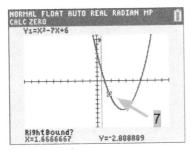

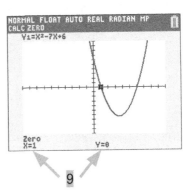

NOTE: You can find a maximum or minimum with the same procedure. In step 5, select:

- "3: minimum" to trace a minimum

- "4: maximum" to trace a maximum

To find a point of intersection

1) Press "y="

2) Input first function into Y1=

3) Input second function into Y2=

4) Press "graph" (both graphs will appear in your window; if they do not, try zooming out by pressing " zoom" and scrolling down to "3: zoom out")

5) Press "2ND" and then "trace"

6) Scroll down to "5: intersect" and press "enter"

7) Move the cursor to a spot near the intersection on t he FIRST curve. Push "enter"

8) Move the cursor to a spot near the intersection on the SECOND curve. Push "enter"

9) Push "enter" a third time

10) The x and y coordinates will appear at the bottom of the screen

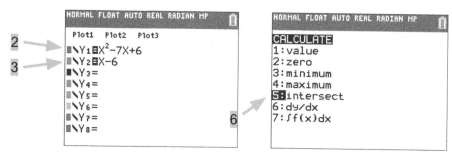

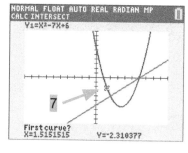
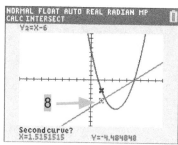

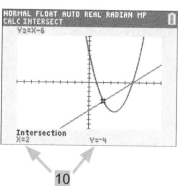

NOTE: This is a great way to solve equations that are difficult to solve by hand.

- Put one side of the equation into Y1=
- Put the other side of the equation into Y2=
- Trace the intersection

NOTE: A great way to test for **equivalency** (without needing to do the algebra) is to use the graphing component. Put one expression into Y1 and the other expression into Y2 and graph them both. If the functions are truly equivalent, they will have the same graphs. They will also have the same table values. Viewing the t able might be quicker than letting the calculator graph the entire functions. To locate a table:

1) Press "2nd"
2) Press "graph"

NORMAL FLOAT AUTO REAL RADIAN MP				
PRESS + FOR △Tbl				
X	Y1	Y2		
9	24	3		
10	36	4		
11	50	5		
12	66	6		
13	84	7		
14	104	8		
15	126	9		
16	150	10		
17	176	11		
18	204	12		
19	234	13		

NOTE: The physical graphs, trace functions, and table values can help you determine several features about a function without needing to perform any operations by hand. You can simply *observe* them. These features include:

1) Y- Intercepts and X- Intercepts (zeros)
2) Maximums & Minimums
3) Points of Intersection
4) Points of Discontinuity
5) Asymptotes
6) Limits
7) Equivalencies to other functions

To find mean, median, and standard deviation for a data set

1) Press "stat" and select "edit"
2) If it is a single list with no frequency, add the values into list 1 (L1)
3) Press "stat" and scroll right to "CALC" menu
4) Select "1-Var Stats"
5) Make sure "Freqlist" is blank and then push "enter" 3 times

  x = mean (average)

  σx = standard deviation

  med = median

6) If the list *does* have a frequency, enter the frequency of each term into list 2 (L2) and continue with steps 3 and 4

7) Scroll down to "FreqList" and input (L2) by pressing "2nd" and the number "2"

8) Press "enter" twice

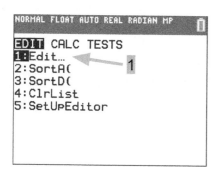

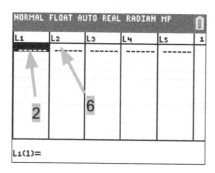

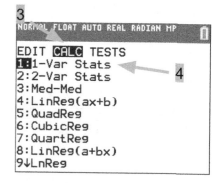

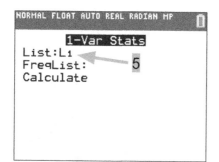

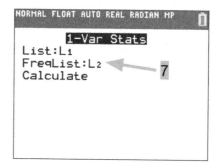

What you will see

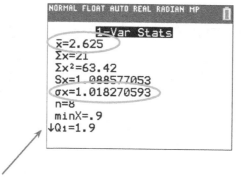

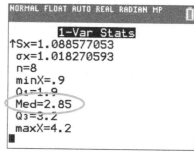

Scroll down to see more information (like the median)

SUMMARY

- Spend the time on the questions that are most likely to award you points.
- Make sure you solidify your basics.
- Use your calculator wisely.
- Double check what the question is asking.
- Re-read the last line of the question AFTER you've completed your calculations.
- Keep track of your variables.
- Circle key words/phrases in the question.
- Pay attention to the order of operations.
- Be very careful with negatives.
- Get comfortable performing basic operations by hand.
- Know how to properly grid-in your answers.
- Start by writing down a formula when you can.
- Step "outside" the problem.
- When in doubt, just start manipulating an expression or equation any way that you can (distribute, factor, combine like terms, cross multiply, ect.).
- You may need to tweak your answer so it matches the available choices.
- Try to eliminate answer choices, even when you don't know how to fully solve a problem.
- Mark up diagrams or draw your own.
- Don't be afraid to play around with the figures they provide.
- Get comfortable translating word problems into equations.
- Look for patterns and identities (like Pythagorean triples).
- Make use of the provided formulas (especially the special triangles)
- Remember that there is often more than one way to solve a problem.
- You can backsolve or use test values if you're truly stuck.

FINAL TIPS

THE NIGHT BEFORE THE EXAM

As crazy as it may sound, you shouldn't study the night before the exam! You may want to briefly review your strategy and formula sheets, but you shouldn't be trying to learn any new information or cram in a lot of last-minute practice. Trust that you have done all you can do. Be confident in what you know, and don't worry about the things that you don't. Most of all, try to relax. That's easier said than done, we know. But these exams are just as much a mental challenge as they are anything else, so it's important that you keep your cool and trust in your instincts!

Here are some things you can do the night before your official exam:

- Read through strategy sheets one last time
- Briefly read through math formula sheet and punctuation sheet
- Make sure you are prepared for exam day

  - **Gather materials.** Make sure you have:
    - Number 2 pencils
    - A calculator (charged and with an extra set of batteries)
    - Your ID and admissions ticket
    - A watch (nothing digital)
    - Water and a snack
  - Have an outfit ready. Dress in layers: you never know how hot or cold your room may be!
  - Make sure you know what location you're going to and how to get there
- Set an alarm
- Set another alarm
- Relax! Don't cram. Do something enjoyable to calm your nerves.
- Get a good night's sleep

THE MORNING OF THE EXAM

- Eat a good breakfast.
- Work through one or two practice problems that you **know how to do** to get your mind working.

- Make sure you have everything you need.
- Stay calm!

RESULTS

You can expect your results within two weeks, **typically 13 days after the exam date**. The one major exception is the June exam, which can take about 5 weeks for scores to be released.

If you take the optional essay, you can expect to see the essay score about 3 days after your multiple choice scores are released.

If you have testing accommodations, you may need to wait longer for your results. There is no designated release date for exams with accommodations, so just hang tight! You may have to wait a few extra weeks, but some students receive their scores just around the time of the standard release date.

At least twice a year, the SAT will give students the option to purchase a **QAS (Question- and- Answer Service) report.** Students will receive a blank copy of the exam and a print-out of their answers. You can access much of this content online as soon as scores are released. This is an incredibly helpful study tool when preparing for future exams. You can sign up to receive this report during the registration process or for several months following the actual exam. Check the CollegeBoard website for up-to-date information on which exams will include this service with and how to register.

1-TO-1 HELP FROM CURVEBREAKERS
Virtual Tutoring

SAT ∘ ACT ∘ SSAT ∘ SHSAT ∘ AP EXAMS ∘ REGENTS
SUBJECT TUTORING ∘ STUDY SKILLS

No matter where you live, connect with a tutor in seconds, and enjoy the flexibility of one-on-one tutoring anywhere with an internet connection.

Curvebreakers is a results-focused company that has a proven track record of success. All of our tutoring plans are customized to the individual student's needs based on our incredibly detailed diagnostic system.

First, we virtually administer a fully timed, previously administered exam to find out your starting point. Our detailed score analysis breaks down the results to make sure each students knows exactly where she needs to focus.

Curvebreakers will formulate a plan based on data and YOU. Through our virtual classroom, we will work with you to take the appropriate and most effective steps you need to improve your score.

Don't waste time with tutors who don't fully understand these exams. Curvebreakers' tutors are required to have scored in the 99th-percentile on the SAT or ACT and are trained in the same flexible and adaptable methodology.

- See How it Works
- Find our package rates
- Contact us with questions
- Watch a Video to learn more!

curvebreakerstestprep.com

Made in the USA
Middletown, DE
06 January 2021